THE BEATLES
FIFTY FABULOUS YEARS

ROBERT RODRIGUEZ

www.G2ent.co.uk

DESIGNERS: Scott Giarnese & Tim Kapustka

PUBLISHERS: Jules Gammond & Edward Adams

PHOTO CREDITS:
AP Images: back cover, end sheets, contents, 8–9, 29, 34, 38–39, 45, 54, 57, 58, 60, 77, 91, 92, 95, 101, 102, 103, 108, 126, 127, 135, 141, 144, 157, 167, 169, 172; Corbis: 41, 65 143; Getty: front cover, 6, 13, 19, 23, 98–99, 121, 132–133. Special thanks to Heritage Auctions. The book's remaining images come from the author's collection.

Library of Congress data available on request

ISBN 978-1-909768-00-0

Printed and bound in China

ROBERT RODRIGUEZ

TABLE OF CONTENTS

INTRODUCTION

Fifty years ago, a group of English youths gathered at a primitive West German recording facility in Hamburg. Both the bassist and drummer from Liverpool's Rory Storm and the Hurricanes joined forces with three members of a rival hometown group, the Beatles, to lay down takes of the standards "Summertime" and "Fever." Though the recording has become lost to history, the strange alchemy produced for the first time that day has not. For on Saturday, October 15, 1960, John Lennon, Paul McCartney, George Harrison, and Ringo Starr recorded together for the first time.

Whatever clicked that day stayed with them, for nearly two years later—just as a record deal beckoned—fate pulled Ringo back into the Beatles' orbit for good. This time the unit jelled, and the music world would never be the same again.

The Beatles' rise to stardom was something more than just another classic rags to riches entertainment story. It possessed particular emotional resonance for millions around the world, a pull that transcended mere recordings. Fans felt connected to the four individuals as people. Though most would never actually meet them, the personalities of the Fab Four were as distinct as any close relative. John was acerbic, irreverent, and rebellious as well as the undisputed leader of the Beatles, at least in the early days. Paul was a natural-born showman—innately gifted at crafting memorable songs that sounded as though they had been around always.

George, the self-styled "dark horse" of the group, provided largely unheralded contributions alongside the dominant two, but his intuitive musicality elevated their catchy ditties to classics. Ringo possessed an "It" factor that made him a star in Liverpool before even joining the band. He had a down-to-earth everyman appeal that earned the praise of his peers and made him the most imitated drummer in rock history.

Though each member was uniquely gifted in his own right, it was as a foursome that they reduced rational people to babbling due to their magnificent music, charisma, and sheer star power. Five decades after the foursome first got together to produce sound, people around the world still cannot get enough of them, sharing their devotion with their families at home and within large gatherings in public.

The Beatles were, and continue to be, as was once said, a force of nature. This is their story.

1960–1963

THE ROAD TO FABNESS

FROM LIVERPOOL TO HAMBURG

"You see, we wanted to be bigger than Elvis."
—John Lennon

On an autumn evening in 1960, a twenty-two-year-old graphic designer named Klaus Voormann quarreled with his girlfriend. The place was Hamburg, West Germany. Though heavily bombed as a vital port city during the war, it now boasted a thriving red-light district known locally as the Reeperbahn. Nothing in Klaus' comfortably middle-class background as a doctor's son and an art student would have familiarized him with the sin strip. But now, in a foul mood, he decided to have a beer in one of the lowlife locale's numerous watering holes.

Lacking any particular destination, he was drawn to a club called the Kaiserkeller. From where he stood on the sidewalk, the racket passing as music emitting from the premises was like catnip to a feline. As an "exi"—one of an artsy crowd of young existentialists— Klaus had no familiarity with rock and roll, being more of a jazz fan. But the sound enthralled him and, against any instincts of caution, he ventured in.

The art crowd avoided the Reeperbahn generally and the dockside clubs specifically, given their reputation for casual violence between transient sailors and the underworld types who populated the area. But once inside, Klaus was transfixed by the act onstage. The group may have struck him as an alien life form: They weren't merely English boys, but *Liverpudlians* besides. Cranking out American rock and roll by the likes of Chuck Berry, Eddie Cochran, and Buddy Holly, the group onstage—Rory Storm and the Hurricanes—featured a lanky, athletic singer as a front man and a sad-faced, bearded drummer. As Klaus later learned, Ringo Starr, as the latter was known, was actually a happy-go-lucky charmer as well as a percussive powerhouse.

On Saturday, July 6, 1957, the Quarry Men played two sets at the Woolton Parish Garden Fete. Hours after this photo was taken, sixteen-year-old John Lennon was introduced to fifteen-year-old Paul McCartney. With that, the 1960s began to take shape.

Klaus took a seat at a table near the stage, sharing it with five youths clad in black-and-white-checked jackets. Their look fascinated him, but no more so than the sound they produced upon taking the stage following the Hurricanes' set. They called themselves the Beatles—a funny name, Klaus thought, with its sonic similarity to German schoolboy slang for the male member. Sporting greased hair piled high atop their heads, they cranked out tunes such as "Sweet Little Sixteen" and "Everybody's Trying to Be My Baby" with abandon, projecting a nothing-left-to-lose vibe, which, in fact, was entirely fitting.

The Beatles—consisting of guitarists John Lennon, Paul McCartney, and George Harrison, as well as drummer Pete Best and novice bass player Stuart Sutcliffe—had landed from across the sea two months earlier. Their "manager," a Liverpool club owner and booking agent named Alan Williams, had made an arrangement with German promoter Bruno Koschmider to supply him with "authentic" English groups for his clubs, which included the Kaiserkeller and the less prestigious Indra Club.Derry and the Seniors arrived earlier that summer, representing some of Liverpool's top-flight club circuit talent. The Beatles, on the other hand, were ranked rather

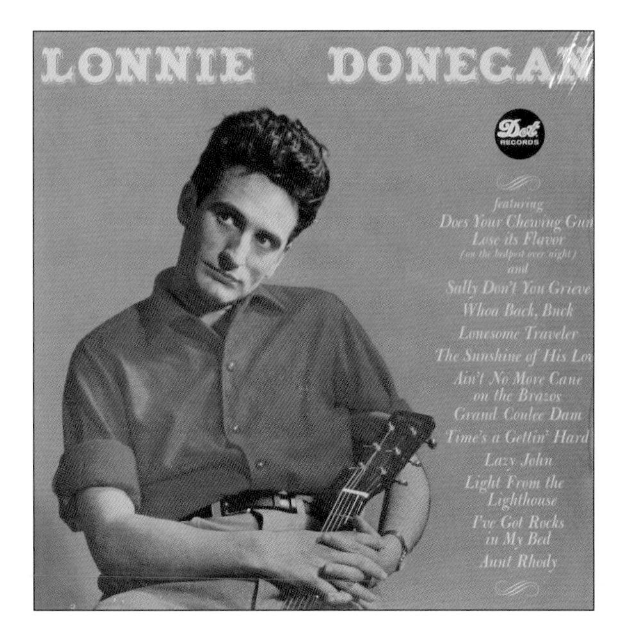

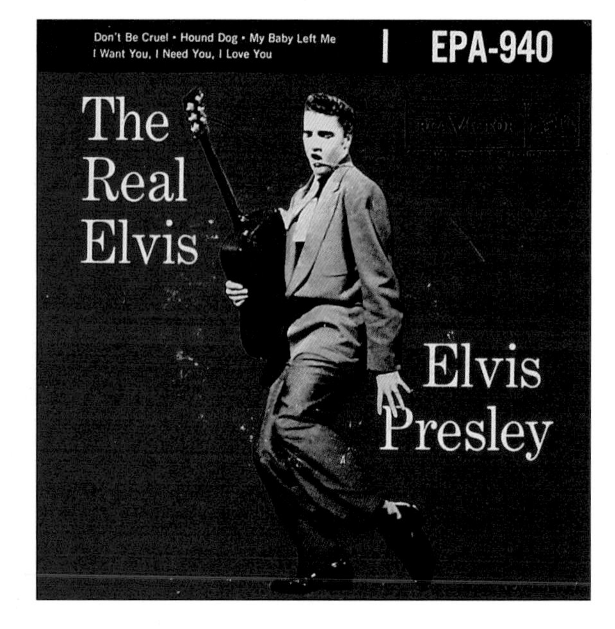

poorly by their peers and only got the booking after Rory Storm turned down the offer.

John Lennon, Paul McCartney, and George Harrison had been playing together since 1958, beginning as a ragtag skiffle outfit dubbed the Quarry Men by John. Like thousands of English teens, he had been inspired to pick up an instrument after the phenomenal success of Lonnie Donegan, purveyor of a hybrid of American blues, country, and folk filtered through an English sensibility. This genre of music was dubbed "skiffle."

With traditional songs like "Rock Island Line" and "Cumberland Gap" among the standard repertoire, skiffle became a left field craze in pre-Elvis Britain in 1956. What made the music appealing to the country's youth was the do-it-yourself ethos. As a genre, skiffle eschewed traditional musicianship and, in fact, was often performed using household objects, such as a

OPPOSITE: Skiffle singer Lonnie Donegan inspired a generation of British children to pick up an instrument to play songs like the ones on this collection. But it was a twenty-one-year-old Memphis truck driver named Elvis Presley who taught the world how to rock with such offerings as this 1956 EP. ABOVE: Seen onstage in the Rainbow Room of the Casbah Club on August 29, 1959, the Quarry Men, with Paul at the mic, entertain a crowd that includes the future Mrs. John Lennon, Cynthia Powell (*center*).

washboard played with finger thimbles scratching out a primitive rhythm. As such, it appealed to those lacking any real ability or an expensive instrument.

Fifteen-year-old John was bowled over by the sound and, with the help of his musically inclined mother, began picking up some modest instrumental skills—mainly banjo chordings, since Julia Lennon did not own a guitar. But it was the reservations of his stern caregiver, Mimi Smith (Julia's elder sister), that John really needed to overcome. At the age of five, John had been placed into the stable domesticity of his aunt and uncle's home, as his mother's rather bohemian lifestyle was judged by Mimi to be too detrimental to serious childrearing. Once John had worn down his aunt's resistance, he acquired a cheap guitar that opened a world of self-expression possibilities. However, Mimi was always quick to remind him, "A guitar's all right, John, but you'll never earn your living with it."

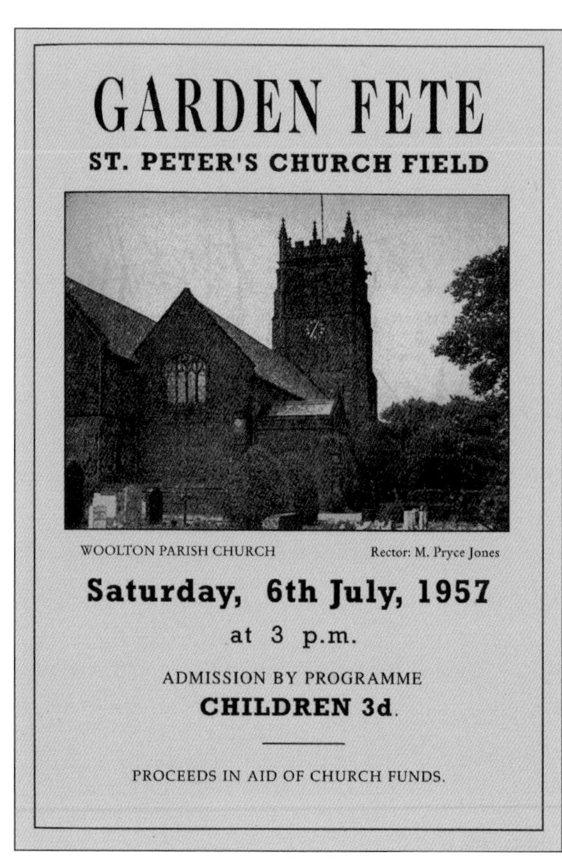

The Quarry Men, so named because its original lineup was drawn from students of Liverpool's Quarry Bank High School, was comprised chiefly of Lennon and his school friends, none of whom possessed any particular musical ability. Still, from their origins in early 1957 through the summer, they had managed to secure a few bookings at parties and street fairs. The biggest event came on a summer Saturday in July: two sets at St. Peter's Church in Woolton. As part of the annual fete, the group competed for attendees' attention alongside a police dog display and the crowning of the Rose Queen.

Present for the festivities was a classmate named Ivan Vaughan. He had brought along a musically inclined mate, fifteen-year-old James Paul McCartney, known to all by his middle name. In the months since his mother succumbed to breast cancer the previous autumn, Paul had thrown himself into an obsessive drive to master the guitar, taking the instrument everywhere while keenly studying American rock and roll singles. Like John by this time, he too had fallen under the spell of the cultural tsunami that was Elvis Presley. Though both youths had individually enjoyed the musical breakthrough that was "Rock Around the Clock," its creator, Bill Haley, was a rather uninspiring figure. Elvis, on the other hand, was a dynamo, possessing the look, the act, and the sound that had turned youth culture on its ear. (An added attraction was the subversive element, as the singer's hypersexual performing style stirred outrage in certain quarters—an irresistible quality to any adolescent.)

Paul was the son of a former bandleader (turned cotton salesman) and grew up in a household in which family sing-alongs beside the piano were commonplace. Above most of his peers, Paul was steeped in a musical environment that was all-inclusive, wherein ragtime, classical, big band, and now rock and roll coexisted. The effects of these varied influences on the boy would become clear as the decade unfolded.

Ivan introduced Lennon and McCartney between sets that afternoon. While Paul was impressed with John's commanding presence and seeming ability to make up his lyrics on the spot (to compensate for forgetting the actual words), John in turn was wowed by Paul's skill set. Not only could he actually *tune* a guitar, but he also seemed to be able to play an unlimited number of rock and roll songs.

OPPOSITE, TOP AND BOTTOM: During their first year, the Quarry Men played mostly parties and the occasional dance. The day that John and Paul met—on July 6, 1957, at Woolton Parish Church in Liverpool—represented their most prestigious booking to date. ABOVE: Had the nascent Quarry Men lived in America, they might have seen many of their rock and roll heroes in one evening, as Alan Freed's *The Biggest Show of Stars for '57* played seventy-eight cities across the country during the fall.

Clinching the deal for the Quarry Men's leader was Paul's performance of Eddie Cochran's "Twenty Flight Rock," a song performed onscreen that year in *The Girl Can't Help It.* Though it took John a few days to think things over, he concluded that strengthening the band was more important than his own position as unquestioned leader.

Moreover, Paul's rock and roll aspirations meshed with his own. The Quarry Men found gigs as a skiffle outfit in such places as the Cavern Club

Fab Fact

The existence of an actual recording of the Quarry Men's set from the day that John and Paul first met was revealed in the early 1990s. Taped by an audience member, the recording was purchased by EMI at an auction for £78,500. However, EMI chose not to release it on the Beatles' *Anthology*, citing the poor quality.

(where rock was forbidden at the time). But John was quick to recognize skiffle's limitations. Once Elvis hit, banging away at "Railroad Bill" no longer seemed terribly appealing. His fellow band members did not share his fervor, if only because it tended to draw the ire of club owners when they slipped "Hound Dog" into the set. But Paul was game, and so now with two dominant figures, the Quarry Men moved further away from their origins as a succession of members came and went.

One addition, brought in by Paul, was fourteen-year-old George Harrison. The "bloody kid," as John initially derided him, possessed undeniable lead guitar chops, remarkable knowledge of chords, and a penchant for working on his parts with monomaniacal intensity. His presence advanced the group's overall sound immeasurably. (Paul himself had aspired to the lead guitar slot, but was doomed by a ham-fisted public performance of Bill Justis' "Raunchy"—a song George replicated with ease.) By spring 1958, three of the future "Fab Four" had found each other.

Throughout that summer and the following year, the Quarry Men studied the sounds emanating from America with far greater intensity than they did their schoolwork. While Elvis remained a firm favorite, other artists also drew their attention. Little Richard was a piano-pounding maniac; his "Long Tall Sally" and "Lucille" quickly found their way into sets, allowing Paul the chance to show off his spot-on impression. Chuck Berry was another early favorite, and his often overlooked skills as a lyricist would influence John profoundly. The close harmonies of the Everly Brothers also left their mark on the group, which soon became renowned for its vocal blend.

But it was Buddy Holly and the Crickets who gave the boys a road map. Holly perfected what became the standard four-man two guitars-bass-drums lineup. Holly also, almost uniquely among his peers, wrote and arranged his own material. Though it took awhile for the Lennon-McCartney songwriting partnership to fully bloom, it was Holly's example that pointed the way to what would really set the Beatles apart, once their success came.

But this was years away, and in 1960, the group, whose number had been joined by Stuart Sutcliffe, an art school pal of John's, found little respect in their hometown. A large part of the disdain stemmed from their chronic inability to hold onto a drummer. Kits were expensive, and few Liverpool youths possessed the wherewithal to own one. (Plus, John later noted, those who did tended to be "idiots.") On more than one occasion, they had to justify their lack of a percussionist by claiming "the rhythm's in the guitars."

Whatever else they had going on, however, the individuals comprising the Quarry Men had persistence. In early 1960, recognizing that skiffle had played out and that any coyness about their rock and roll aspirations fooled no one, they decided upon a name change. Infatuation with Holly's Crickets as well as Lennon's fondness for puns prompted Sutcliffe, the newest member, to suggest Beatals. In addition to the insect connotation, rock and roll was known locally as "beat music." John and the others liked the suggestion, but not without further tweaking. In May they became the Silver Beetles, but by August this evolved to simply the Beatles. (This provided a further unintentional pun, as their ongoing drummer issues meant that they were often "beat-less.")

Though few around them would take the claim seriously, the course was now set for the Beatles to one day fulfill their stated ambition: to be "bigger than Elvis."

OPPOSITE: Beyond Elvis and Buddy Holly, Chuck Berry was another profound influence on the young Quarry Men. In 1972, Berry would perform with a still-starstruck John Lennon on TV's *Mike Douglas Show.* ABOVE: In the final months of 1960, the Beatles' stage act grew by leaps and bounds, spurred by competition with Rory Storm and the Hurricanes. The two bands shared the bill at the *Kaiserkellar.*

THE SOUND OF BRITISH YOUTH

"Mach schau, Beatles! Mach schau!"
—Kaiserkellar *club owner Bruno Koschmider*

The American incursion into the consciousness of British youth went unreciprocated in the early 1960s. Though exports from the former colony were being absorbed by Brits as quickly as they crossed the ocean, success of British rock acts on *this* side of the pond was virtually nonexistent, beyond a small number of one-hit wonders: Lonnie Donegan, Cliff Richard, Helen Shapiro, the Tornadoes. Americans simply did not have the taste for anything "foreign" just yet, and this attitude fostered an inferiority complex among the Brit entertainers who kept trying for that elusive opening.

Back in Liverpool, there was no shortage of talent hoping to break past local stardom. Of them, only one actually succeeded. Billy Fury (born Ronald Wycherley) had been a Merseyside dockworker, but his real ambition was to make it as a songwriter. His smoldering good looks and raw charisma made him the closest thing England had to its own Elvis. A suggestive stage act and film and TV appearances helped propel a string of Fury hits up the charts.

In May 1960, the newly dubbed Silver Beetles actually auditioned to replace Fury's departed backing band. Featuring the twin rhythm guitars of John and Paul, George on lead, a thirty-six-year-old forklift driver named Tommy Moore on drums, and Stuart Sutcliffe, an art school buddy of John's, on bass, the band's professional experiences to this point had been mostly confined to local dance halls. It took tremendous cheek to even appear in a setting where they were so outclassed, but John, at least, justified the occasion by securing the singer's autograph.

Shown here in 1961 at the Top Ten Club during their second Hamburg stint, the Beatles had evolved into a powerhouse band by this time. Prior to John and Paul's emerging songwriting abilities, George often sang lead with their cover-heavy sets.

ABOVE: The five-man Beatles, pre-leather, play in the fall of 1960 upon their arrival in Hamburg. Foreshadowing his fate, Pete Best alone lacks a matching jacket. OPPOSITE, TOP: Liverpool's Billy Fury was the local boy who made it big, appearing often on TV as well as in a feature film built around him, 1962's *Play It Cool*. It costarred Helen Shapiro, with whom the Beatles would tour in 1963. OPPOSITE, BOTTOM: Rory Storm and the Hurricanes, pictured circa 1960, were thoroughly seasoned professionals compared to the rough-and-tumble Beatles. But a lack of success on vinyl led to their eclipse by other Liverpool acts.

It often has been suggested that the band failed to impress due to the ineptitude of its novice bassist, who, it is said, was so hopelessly unskilled that he would perform with his back to the audience, lest anyone notice his fumbling incompetency. The facts suggest otherwise: Though the top prize did not go to the Silver Beetles—or any Liverpool act present (London's Tornados got the gig)—Lennon and company were hired to back another Parnes act, Johnny Gentle, on an excursion into Scotland.

It's true that Sutcliffe was a beginner musically, but he *did* manage to master a primitive but driving undercurrent, roughly akin to what today we'd call "punk." In any event, the story that Parnes was prepared to hire the Silver Beetles to back Fury only if they dumped their bassist amounts to after-the-fact mythmaking.

The weeklong Gentle jaunt gave the group its first taste of "touring" as well as big-time show business experience, as they played before audiences in theaters rather than clubs or coffee bars. It left them hungry for more, which came soon enough in the form of an offer not even intended for them. Alan Williams, a local bar owner and promoter, had lucked into becoming Hamburg's go-to person in Liverpool for booking bands. After Derry and the Seniors became a hit at Bruno Koschmider's *Kaiserkellar*, Williams requested more of the same for another venue, the Indra Club.

Williams' first choice, Rory Storm, was booked through summer. Only with the greatest reluctance did he agree to send the Beatles, on the condition that they secure a permanent drummer. (Moore retired after a month with the group, weary of their dismal prospects and Lennon's unceasing abuse.) Backed into a corner, the Beatles prevailed upon Pete Best, the son of a Liverpool club owner, to join them in order to get the gig. Best agreed, and the group, now officially The Beatles, took a giant leap into the unknown.

After a brief stint at the Indra Club, the Beatles were sent to the *Kaiserkeller,* where they joined the by-now-arrived Rory Storm (who was top-billed). Contractually, they were bound to play seven nights a week for a total of nearly forty hours. Lest their energies flag, Koschmider was quick to exhort them: *"Mach schau! Mach schau!"* This roughly translated to "Fire it up for the paying audience!" The boys were therefore expected to pull out all the stops to keep the drunks entertained. (Should this fail to provide enough incentive, friendly waiters were always on hand to ply them with amphetamines and beer.)

Despite, or more likely because of, how hard they were pushed, the Hamburg experience transformed the Beatles from rudderless wannabes to a high-energy act that thrived on working an audience. Every ounce of imagination they possessed was channeled into taking command of the room, from their routine baiting of the crowd ("Nazis!") to discovering musical invention they didn't know they possessed while playing two-minute songs for twenty-minute stretches.

On October 15, 1960, John, Paul, and George were joined by Ringo Starr (and a Hurricanes singer named Wally) in a demo studio, where they laid down a few tracks. Though the tape no longer exists, a handful of listeners were given their first taste of a sound that would soon trigger a revolution in music—and in youth culture.

THE FIFTH BEATLES

"I would like to look after them in some way throughout their lives, not because I want a percentage but because they are my friends."
—Brian Epstein

As the man who sent the nascent Beatles to Hamburg (and therefore on their way), Alan Williams served as the band's first essential mentor. But it is beyond argument that their ascent to worldwide superstardom would not have occurred at all were it not for the roles played by two key figures: their manager, Brian Epstein, and their producer, George Martin. Both men saw (and heard) in the group something that eluded all other observers in position to further their progress. To their credit, they took on the Beatles, each in effect becoming a "fifth" key member.

The Beatles' initial Hamburg stint ended ingloriously in December 1960 after they incurred Bruno Koschmider's wrath. After the band broke its contract to accept an offer at Peter Eckhorn's more prestigious Top Ten Club, Koschmider didn't hesitate to exact his revenge. First, he tipped off authorities that George, seventeen, was under age, leading to his immediate deportation. Further, he filed a complaint for attempted arson against Paul and Pete, resulting in their arrest. (The two had scorched a wall by igniting a condom to serve as light while they packed their things.)

One by one, the Beatles dragged themselves back home, elated at their own progress while feeling ashamed that the trip, which had started out with such hope, had ended so ignominiously. Any feelings of self-pity were shaken off by their return engagement at Litherland Town Hall in December. Though playing in their hometown, their billing as "direct from Hamburg" fooled some into believing that the larger-than-life specter—they were clad in leather and cowboy boots—really was the vanguard of a Teutonic invasion.

Producer George Martin's role in the Beatles' career was every bit as vital as Brian Epstein's. He was on hand in April 1963 when the group received the first of many sales awards, this one a silver disc for the "Please Please Me" single.

History records that the Beatles knocked 'em dead that night.

They returned to Hamburg the following spring, basically picking up where they'd left off. The star of the *Reeperbahn* strip was a fellow Brit named Tony Sheridan, who offered up a dynamic set of American rock and roll, represented with an English twist. He and the Beatles struck up a friendship, which culminated in June with the group being asked to back Sheridan on some recording dates. (Stuart Sutcliffe, meanwhile, had decided to retire from the group to resume his art studies, resulting in Paul shifting to bass.)

Produced by German music mogul Bert Kaempfert (co-writer of "Strangers in the Night"), the session produced rave-up versions of the chestnuts "My Bonnie (Lies Over the Ocean)" and "The Saints," as well as a pair of tracks featuring the group without Sheridan: an instrumental (co-credited to John and George) entitled "Cry for a Shadow" and a take on the 1927 standard "Ain't She Sweet," sung by John.

"My Bonnie" was issued in Germany (where it peaked on the charts at No. 5) in October 1961. Word that the Beatles had cut a record reached England, where they had established a residency at Liverpool's Cavern Club. The record, available as an import, drew notice from fans, including one who placed an order for the single at a shop located just yards away from the club. The shop's manager, twenty-seven-year-old Brian Epstein, prided himself on customer satisfaction. Though the Beatles were regulars at his store and appeared inside issues of the musical paper *Mersey Beat,* published by their friend Bill Harry and on sale at NEMS (North End Music Store), Epstein would later claim ignorance of their existence.

ABOVE: Possessing a flair for presentation and dogged tenacity, Brian Epstein had the drive to make the Beatles "bigger than Elvis." He would bring them success on a scale greater than anyone had dared imagine. OPPOSITE, TOP: Recorded in June 1961, "My Bonnie," featuring Tony Sheridan and the Beatles (albeit as the "Beat Brothers"), brought the group that had operated right under his nose to Brian's attention. OPPOSITE, BOTTOM: Bill Harry, an art college friend of John's, published *Mersey Beat,* a local music periodical that boosted the Beatles' career in the pre-fame days.

If one takes his version as gospel, then perhaps confusion over the connection between the "My Bonnie" single and the group known locally is valid. After all, it was a German record, on which they were credited as "the Beat Brothers" (to avoid their real name's unsavory association) rather than

"Guitar groups are on the way out, Mr. Epstein."

—Decca executive Dick Rowe in turning down the Beatles in early 1962, a year before signing the Rolling Stones

by their official moniker. To clarify issues, Epstein paid a visit to the Cavern himself, catching a lunchtime session on November 9. Unlike most in position to help them, he was knocked out by their presence and the apparent sway they held over the hundreds of kids packed into the rather squalid subterranean venue.

His own need for both a challenge and an outlet for his gift for presentation led to their striking an agreement one month after meeting: Brian would serve as their manager, securing more prestigious bookings and, ultimately, a recording contract. The Beatles in turn would smarten up their act. They would ditch the leather and their rough-and-ready performance style in favor of tailored suits and clockwork precision with their sets. If they were to win over the masses and fulfill their ambitions to become "bigger than Elvis," some fundamental changes would be necessary.

MERSEY BEAT

O.P.B.

MERSEYSIDE TOPS

MERSEYSIDE'S ONLY PUBLISHED TOP TWENTY

Beatles Head Merseyside Tops

TED EASTON

ALLEN BROS. : 33 ORRELL LANE

AUDREY'S—

HAIR STYLISTS

SPECIAL OFFER TO READERS

3A SONO ST. • LIVERPOOL • NOR 0375

TEEN BEAT NIGHT

RECORD SESSIONS

CRANE THEATRE

Every Friday

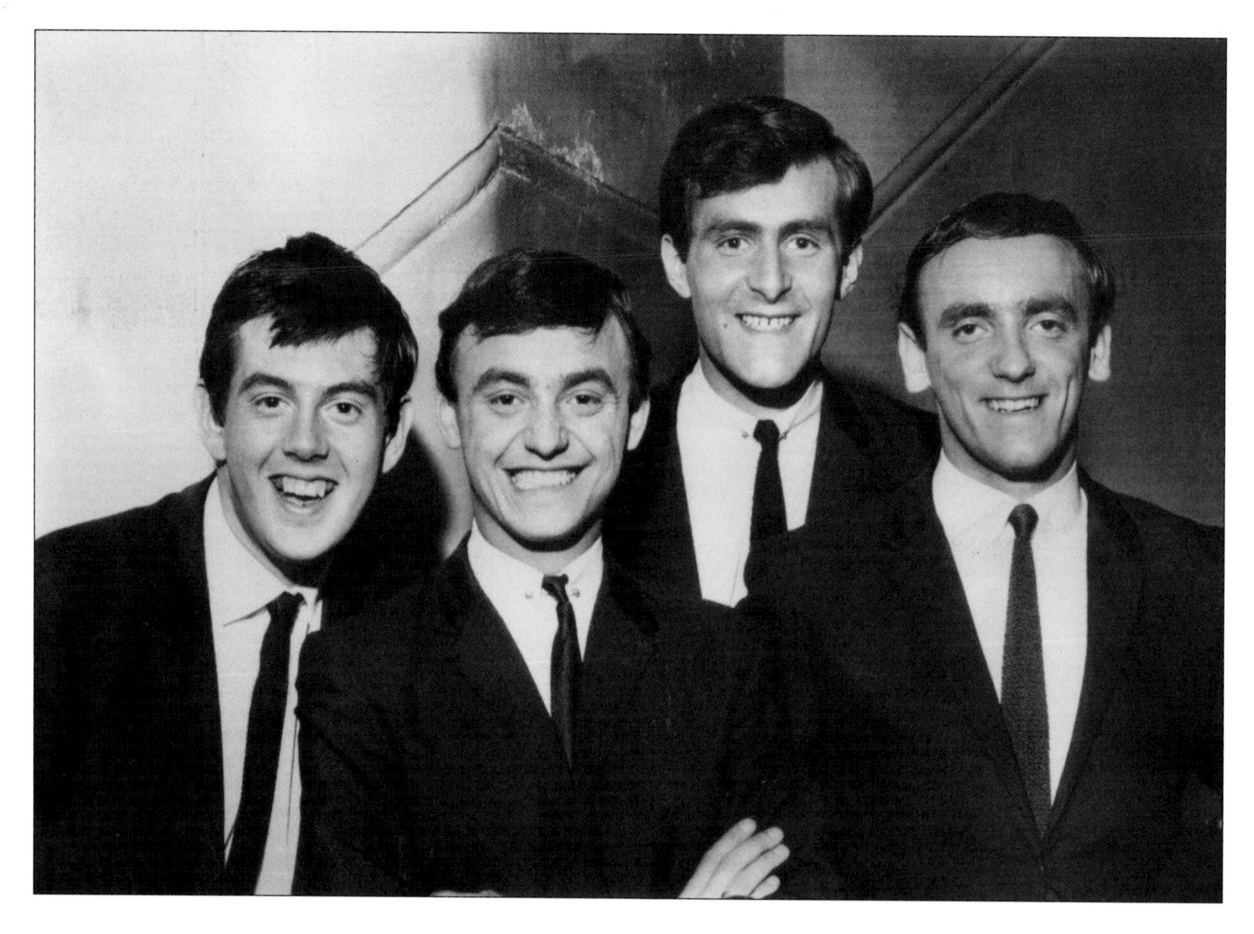

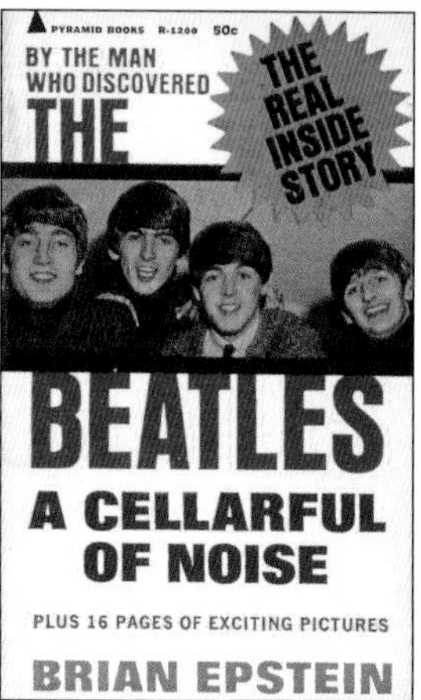

Epstein also had some pull within the industry. As a retailer managing some nine record stores, his word commanded attention with record companies. Underscoring his commitment, Brian arranged for an audition with the powerful Decca Records label down in London on New Year's Day, 1962, just a few weeks after inking a deal with the boys. Dazzled by the sudden upswing in their fortunes, the Beatles made the long journey outside their comfort zone, lugging their tatty gear south, filled with hope.

They arrived slightly the worse for wear, being a little hung over from celebrations the night before, knackered, and more than a little in awe of their surroundings. What has famously become known as "the Decca audition tape" documents a band with flashes of brilliance (note John's vocal on "Hello Little Girl" or Paul's compositional skills on the inexplicably still-unreleased "Love of the Loved"). Yet they were brought down by palpable nervousness, a set that sacrificed their originals in favor of too many novelty tunes (selected by Brian to showcase their versatility), and a club-footed drummer. (What may have worked in a live setting came off as painfully ham-fisted within the confines of a studio.)

Unsurprisingly, the label turned them down—a decision viewed through the years as one of history's all-time blunders. In fact, it was ultimately for the better. Had they been signed as is, the Beatles would have been hindered by Pete Best's shortcomings over the long haul. Furthermore, there is little reason to believe that they would have ended up in the hands of so nurturing and visionary a producer as the one they would eventually land: George Martin.

In his own way (and especially in view of later accomplishments), Martin's path of underachieving paralleled that of the group's. He was a staff producer at Parlophone, regarded as EMI's weak sister within its larger scope of labels. Martin was classically trained, but his reputation stemmed largely from the success of the comedy records he had produced with The Goons (featuring Peter Sellers and enjoyed tremendously by the Beatles). Though he had produced his share of pop and jazz records, rock and roll on the order of what the Beatles were cranking out was beyond his ken.

After literally exhausting all other record company possibilities throughout early 1962, Epstein finally managed to win an audience with Martin, who agreed to hear the group at EMI's recording facility, located on Abbey Road in London. The actual meeting took place on June 6. Though the music struck Martin as nothing special, their personalities and wit *did* win him over. (He may also have recognized that with a prevailing royalty rate of a penny per record, he wasn't exactly putting his employer's fortune at risk, should the group bomb.)

Martin offered them a contract to produce an initial single in late summer. The first order of business, though, was to do something about that drummer.

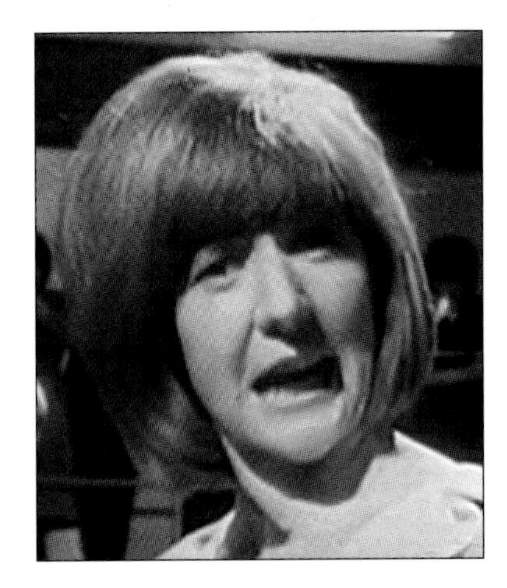

Fab Fact

The group's final stint in Hamburg, at the newly opened Star Club, was taped by musician Ted Taylor. (Permission was secured in exchange for a case of beer.) Though the Beatles and Brian Epstein took a pass on buying the recordings, they eventually saw issue in 1977 as a double LP, *Live! at the Star-Club in Hamburg, Germany; 1962*.

OPPOSITE, TOP: Gerry and the Pacemakers, another band from Liverpool, actually beat the Beatles to a national No. 1 with the song the latter group rejected, "How Do You Do It." The two acts shared the same manager and producer. OPPOSITE, BOTTOM: Brian Epstein's autobiography, *A Cellarful of Noise,* was ghostwritten by Derek Taylor, a journalist at the time but eventually the Beatles' press officer and close friend. ABOVE: Cilla Black followed the trail that the Beatles blazed, as she shared their manager and recorded Lennon-McCartney originals with George Martin.

BEATLEMANIA

"Gentlemen, you've just made your first No. 1 record."
—George Martin, right after the group nailed
a take of "Please Please Me"

When Pete Best joined the Beatles in 1960 in order to facilitate their employment in Hamburg, it was largely a marriage of convenience. For Pete, it was a step up for his career. It gave him the chance to play outside the confines of the Liverpool club (The Casbah) that his mother, Mona, operated in their basement, and it gave him the opportunity to sow some wild oats abroad. But although the somewhat taciturn drummer readily bonded with his bandmates, there always seemed to be an "other" characteristic that typified relations between them.

To begin with, Pete rarely socialized with the other three; he frequently was off on his own somewhere during their downtime. Compelled by his role in the band to be at the back of the stage, he therefore wasn't well placed to cut up with the others. (However, he did get the chance to play front man as singer during performances of "Peppermint Twist" while Paul took over the skins.) His inability to adopt the uniform hairstyle now worn by the other three couldn't have helped, though this stemmed more from physiology than obstinacy.

While his skills were at least adequate for their raucous stage presentation, it may have been George Martin's less than glowing assessment that sealed his fate. With a recording career and everything they had worked for to this point hanging in the balance, Lennon, McCartney, and Harrison were not about to let sentiment stand in the way of fulfilling their musical ambitions. (Another seldom-discussed factor may have been forty-year-old Mona Best giving birth to a baby in July 1962, fathered by the Beatles' nineteen-year-old roadie, Neil Aspinall. Brian Epstein's control of the band's image

The eruption of Beatlemania in the fall of 1963 ensured that never again would the public get as close to the group as this Swedish fan did in Stockholm on October 26.

ABOVE: "Love Me Do," the first record issued under their own name, wasn't exactly musically groundbreaking but it did put the Beatles on the map. Its follow-up, the infectious "Please Please Me," assured observers that their success was no fluke.

was total, and with word of John's marriage being kept under lock and key, certainly a story far more salacious could have been seen as a death blow of scandal.)

The Beatles already had a replacement in mind: Richard Starkey, known professionally as Ringo Starr. As drummer with Rory Storm and the Hurricanes, he was already celebrated locally as both a creative and powerful drummer and as a performer. ("Ringo Starrtime," a solo vignette, was a feature of their sets.) Moreover, the Beatles and Ringo had bonded in Hamburg, drinking and carousing together, as the drummer possessed a quick wit on par with the rest of them. He and George were particularly close, and it was the guitarist who pushed the hardest to switch drummers.

In August 1962, it fell to Brian Epstein to do the dirty work, a job he relished not one bit. A shocked Pete Best was forced to move on to a more mundane life as he watched his former group zoom into the stratosphere. As for Ringo, the starring vehicle that had been predicted for him by virtually all who knew him had at last arrived. He slid comfortably into the role, though acceptance of the switch by the group's fans was not immediate. Best had his partisans, and even George Martin was stunned that the band member he felt was the best looking should have been summarily dismissed. (He would later assert that his criticism of Best's drumming was not meant as a directive. He felt that session drummers could fill Best's role on records while the group dynamic stayed intact. Mostly, he feared being blamed.)

When the time came to lay down that first single at EMI, Martin appreciated the group's enthusiasm for its own material while not sharing it. Recognizing the importance of a debut record, he felt that a tune written by a professional would make a better impression. Their first clash of wills resulted in the Beatles recording a half-hearted version of Mitch Murray's "How Do You Do It," after which Martin recognized the futility of pushing them where they did not want to go. Of the material they presented, he judged "Love Me Do," an adolescent expression of Tin Pan Alley moon-June sentiments, to be the best of the lot.

Still, he wasn't prepared to take any chances with an untested new drummer. One week after the group laid down a performance that Martin was certain could be bettered, Ringo showed up for a retake, only to find studio pro Andy White in his place. The stunned newcomer was shunted to tambourine duties, feeling that he'd been Pete bested. The Ringo-less performance was ultimately chosen for album release, though *his* take did see issue as a single.

Powered by John's harmonica riffing and being more of a throwback to their skiffle days than their typical set material, "Love Me Do" (released on October 5, 1962) was nonetheless a huge achievement. Billy Fury notwithstanding, the song's peak at No. 17 on the national charts showed that self-penned material from a group originating from the sticks could compete alongside American rock acts on the national stage in Britain.

The success came as the group prepared to play its last club dates in Hamburg, the city that served as its crucible. During the holiday season in 1962, they were top billed at the newly opened Star Club. The end of the year marked a major turning point for a band that literally had been turned down by every record label in England. Now they had a deal and a Top 20 hit. Some adjustments had been effected to bring about the change in fortunes, notably the drummer switch but also their image. Clad in matching tailored stage wear, the Beatles became trendsetters (for the first of many times) under Brian Epstein's unerring eye.

It would be their haircuts that largely distinguished them before the public, especially in America. Back when Klaus Voormann had first laid eyes on them, the group evoked a sort of Tony Curtis/Elvis Presley throwback look, necessitating the use of much hair grease. But Stuart Sutcliffe soon took up with Klaus's ex-girlfriend, Astrid Kirchherr. Her influence on him, the Beatles—and by extension, Western culture—was profound.

Stuart began wearing his hair combed forward in the style of French students, favored by Astrid. After initial mockery, John, Paul, and George eventually took up the cut themselves, though Pete's naturally wavy locks refused to be tamed. As for Stuart, the promising art student became engaged to Astrid, but he tragically died of a cerebral hemorrhage just days before his former band was to arrive for its third Hamburg hitch in April 1962. He was twenty-one.

"And then one day—it was in August 1962—John Lennon called me and he said, 'You're in, shave your beard'—I had a beard again—'but keep your sidies.' That's sideburns, you know."

—Ringo Starr, on his induction into the Beatles

ABOVE and OPPOSITE BOTTOM: The Beatles' fashion sense brought them almost as much attention as their music. Their novel hairstyles also drew notice, especially in a crew-cutted and Brylcreemed America. Products such as this Beatles hair pomade assured purchasers that they too could become fashionably up-to-date. OPPOSITE TOP: The LP *Please Please Me* was released in Great Britain on March 22, 1963.

With one hit under their belt, George Martin and EMI were anxious for a follow-up, lest interest in the band of unknowns evaporate. John and Paul were quick to nominate a Lennon composition inspired by both Roy Orbison and songs from the 1940s that John's mother used to sing to him. "Please Please Me" began life as a loping ballad, failing to impress their producer. He suggested speeding up the tempo. With the faster pace and the addition of a dynamic call-and-response vocal line, the song possessed exactly the right amount of seductive charm to send anyone's adrenalin pumping. (No one challenged Ringo's prowess from this point forward, either.)

Released in January 1963, the song benefited from the Beatles' availability to actively promote it (live, on TV, and on the radio), since they had fulfilled their Hamburg obligations. "Please Please Me" rocketed up the charts, but before it reached the top slot in *New Musical Express* and *Melody Maker,* the boys were whisked back into the studio to produce an album in order to capitalize on the success. While EMI was still uncertain of their long-term prospects, they were willing to spring for studio time to lay down enough tracks to fill a long player—as long as they completed their work in a day.

Please Please Me, the LP, was recorded on February 11, 1963. History records this as perhaps one of the most productive days in rock. Ten songs were laid

down (bolstered by the four cuts representing the A and B sides of their two singles). Among them were the timeless "I Saw Her Standing There," a Paul composition inspired by Chuck Berry; "Do You Want to Know a Secret," written for George by John; "Boys," an inspired girl group song custom, tailored as a showcase for Ringo; and "Twist and Shout," a raw rocker that taxed John's vocal chords to their very limit. (Both John and Paul were suffering from head colds that day; that they acquitted themselves as well as they did was a minor miracle.)

The album was rush released in March, by which time they had recorded a third single, "From Me to You," famously written by John and Paul on the bus between gigs on their first national tour. Perhaps fueled by the burgeoning eruption of fandom in the third single's wake, *Please Please Me* made it to No. 1 on the LP charts in May and, remarkably, stayed at the top spot until

Fab Fact

After his dismissal, Pete Best only once encountered his former band, at a Cavern gig in February 1963. Both parties took pains to avoid the other after that, although in 1967 John Lennon borrowed military medals belonging to Mona Best's father to wear on the cover of *Sgt. Pepper*.

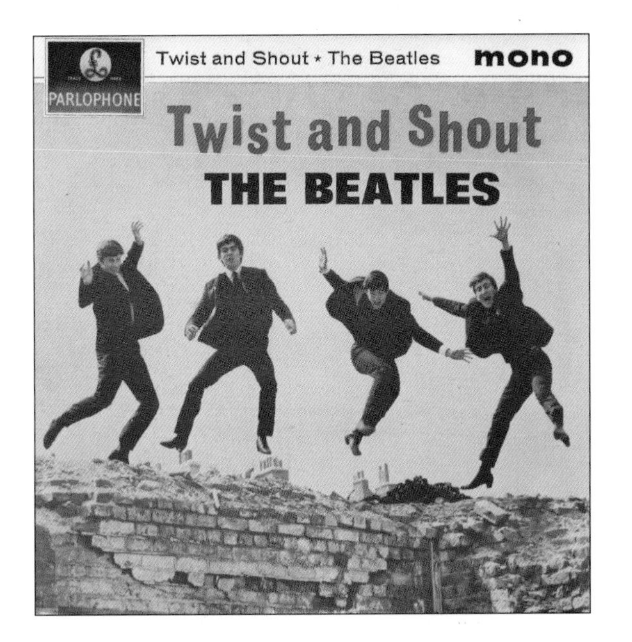

November. (It was finally dislodged by, of all things, their follow-up: *With the Beatles.*) "From Me to You" also hit No. 1, as did their summer of '63 single, "She Loves You." This last song, with its insistent "yeah, yeah, yeah" refrain, caught the public's imagination as powerfully as did the group's hair.

As a part of the makeover from gritty club act to TV-ready recording stars, Brian's strategy included placing them in support roles for some high-profile acts touring the country. By spreading their brand throughout the homeland, they managed to sell some records while hitching their wagon to celebrity larger than their own. The first that year came as opening act for sixteen-year-old Helen Shapiro, a big-voiced singer whose "Walkin' Back to Happiness" went to No. 1 in England (while stalling at 100 in the States). Recognizing early on the potential windfall that came from a successful cover, John and Paul wasted no opportunity in crafting a tune for Helen, "Misery," which was rebuffed by her management without her even hearing it.

Meanwhile, others began to recognize the quality of the Lennon-McCartney songbook (or as it was initially billed, McCartney-Lennon). Among them was singer Billy J. Kramer, a client of Brian Epstein's, whose recording of "Bad to Me," written by John, went to No. 1 in August. Cilla Black, a

OPPOSITE: Try as he might, this young PC could not block out the screams of these Manchester fans, two days before the Beatles' second album was issued. ABOVE: If anyone in England still didn't own *Please Please Me* by summer 1963, they could purchase four songs from it on the *Twist and Shout* EP. A bounty of new material arrived in November on *With the Beatles,* their second long-player.

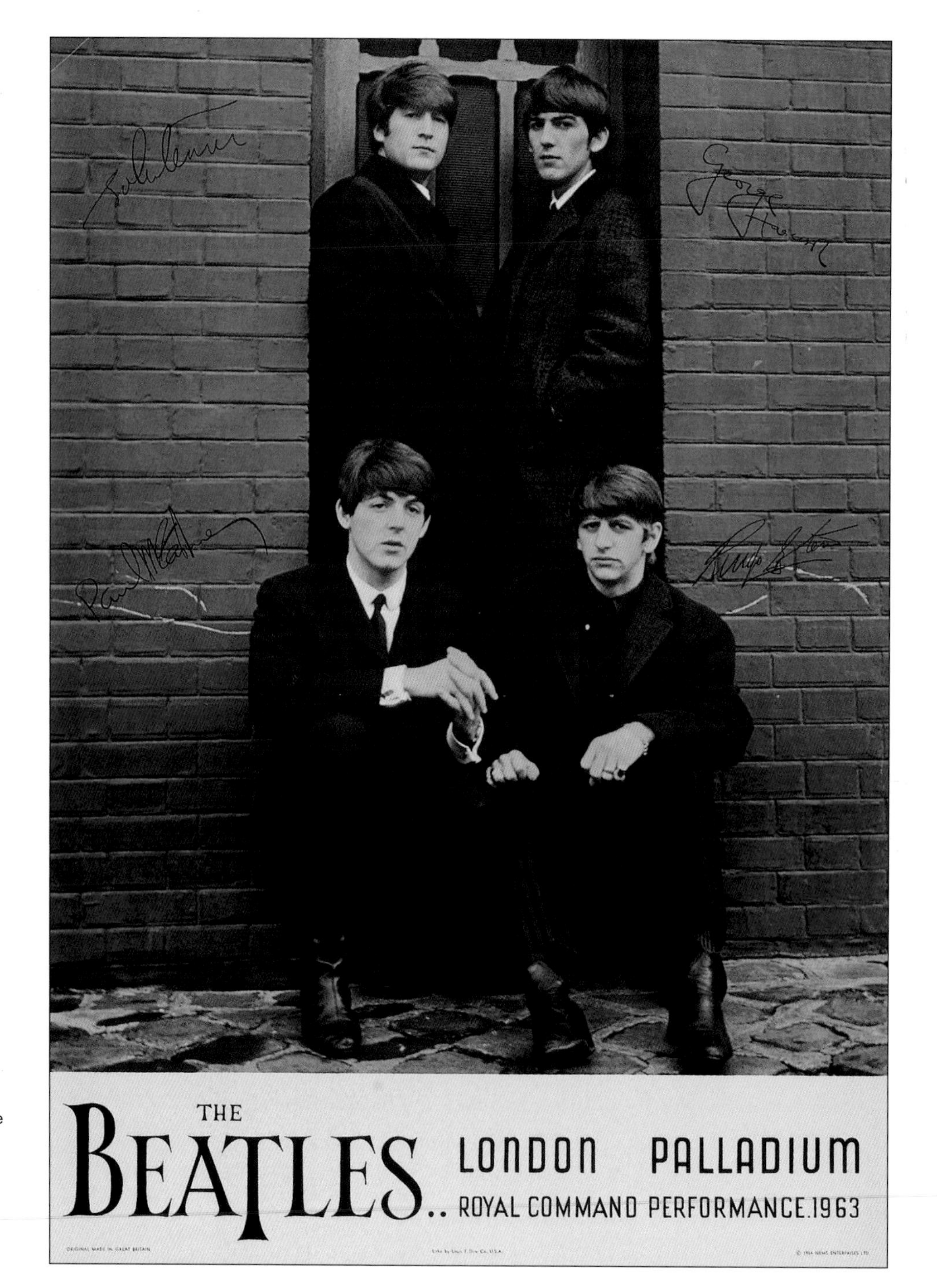

RIGHT and OPPOSITE, TOP: This poster and newsstand special commemorated both Beatles blockbuster shows from the fall of 1963. OPPOSITE, BOTTOM: The high-octane ratings of Ed Sullivan's Sunday night program made it the ideal showcase for turning unknowns into stars overnight. He is seen here with Topo Gigio, "the Italian mouse"—a sensation nearly as big as the Beatles during the 1960s.

former hatcheck girl at the Cavern Club, was another Epstein act. She debuted with "Love of the Loved," another tune left unrecorded for EMI by the Beatles. Also, American singer Del Shannon ("Runaway") recorded "From Me to You."

The Beatles' early-1963 national tours came alongside singers Chris Montez ("Let's Dance") and Tommy Roe ("Sheila") and, in the spring, Roy Orbison. The burgeoning mania that accompanied the group's portion of the concerts led to some embarrassment, as audiences began giving a far greater reception to them than they did the headliners. Never before had a homegrown act drawn bigger accolades than established American stars.

Autumn 1963 saw a pair of high-profile gigs seal the group's official ascension to phenomenon. On October 13—just two months after taking their final bow at the Cavern—the Beatles were top-billed on *Sunday Night at the London Palladium,* the highest-rated variety show on British television. The resulting fan hysteria (both in and outside the theater), at last penetrating the public's consciousness, was dubbed "Beatlemania." Just weeks later, they were featured at the Royal Command Performance, this time before an audience that included the Queen Mother and Princess Margaret. John's cheeky admonition to those in the expensive seats to "rattle your jewelry" bought them some press, characterizing the group as irreverent and fun.

Between these two dates, the Beatles returned from a brief jaunt to Sweden. The reception from the fans greeting their return at the airport in London was riotous. Among the innocent bystanders witnessing the tremendous outpouring of emotion was American television variety show host Ed Sullivan. Though completely ignorant of the band and its music, he recognized a phenomenon when he saw it, likening it to the hysteria that accompanied the rise of Elvis Presley. He made a mental note to himself to find out who these young men were and, if possible, book them for his show.

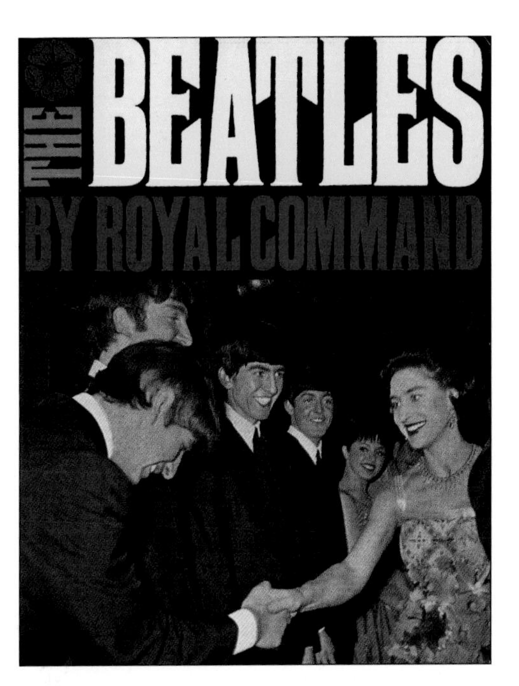

1964–1965

BIGGER THAN ELVIS

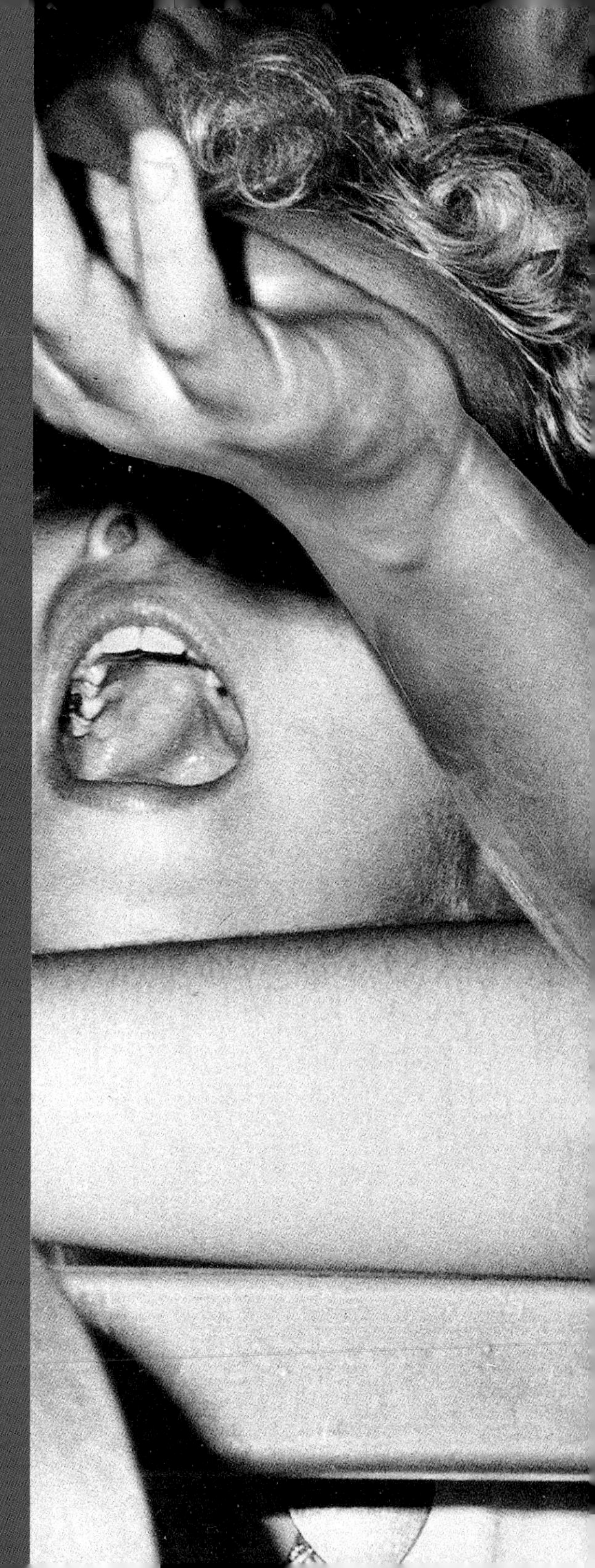

I
LOVE
RINGO

THE AMERICAN SOUND

"We knew that America would make us or break us as world stars. In fact, she made us."
—Brian Epstein

In a rather gross generalization, it has been said that the three years or so before the Beatles hit were a rather fallow period for rock and roll. The early 1960s, we've been told, was the valley between the pioneering peaks of Elvis, Chuck Berry, Little Richard, and Buddy Holly in the 1950s and the eruption of Beatlemania in 1963-64. Rock's principles had either died (Holly, Eddie Cochran), gone into the army (Elvis, Everly Brothers), were in jail (Berry), or found God (Little Richard), paving the way for the rise of pretty-boy acts such as Frankie Avalon and Fabian. In reality, the field flourished with dozens of stars producing timeless music during those years, much of it absorbed by the Beatles, who—as always—kept close tabs on American sounds.

While Elvis inspired them to rock in the first place, musically his influence paled alongside that of his contemporaries. (Beatles covers of his material were uncommon, although the ballad "Love Me Tender" was crooned by Stuart Sutcliffe during their Hamburg years.) More influential was Elvis' Sun Records colleague, Carl Perkins, who—in addition to his rockabilly guitar stylings—produced several songs that became staples of the Beatles' sets. Three of them would be recorded by the band, including "Matchbox" and "Honey Don't."

Just one year after touring as American star Roy Orbison's support act, the Beatles, seen here celebrating the singer's twenty-eight birthday in April 1964, were on top of the world. Years later, George and Roy would join forces in a supergroup dubbed the Traveling Wilburys.

The boys also eagerly absorbed the assembly line soul emanating from Detroit. Both as a singer and songwriter, Smokey Robinson was especially influential. (As a solo artist, George would record *two* tributes to the Motown legend.) R&B was a staple of the Beatles' listening habits, as were country and pop, the latter epitomized by the rise of the so-called Brill Building

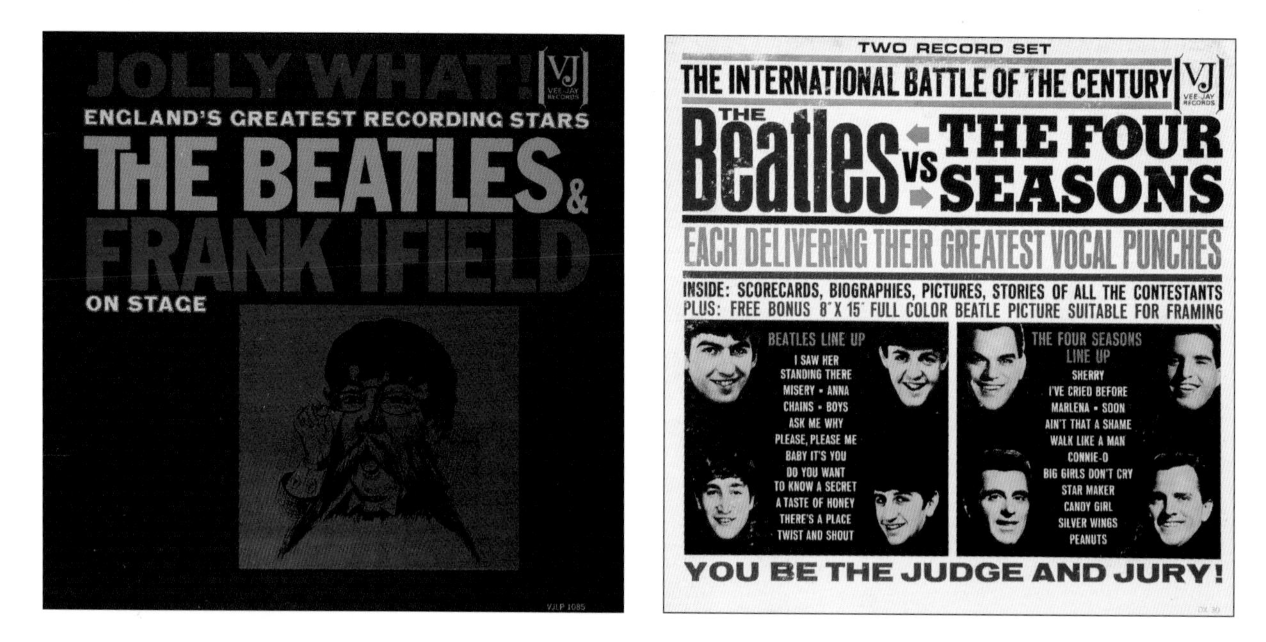

Facing the loss of the Beatles' recordings to Capitol, Vee-Jay Records made hay while the sun shined, cranking out releases of questionable value to consumers while endlessly recycling the handful of tunes that they held the rights to.

sound. This was a New York City locale inhabited by platoons of professional songwriters and music publishers who cranked out hits by the dozen.

Artists ranging in diversity from Gene Pitney to Little Eva scored hit after hit with tunes knocked out by the likes of Neil Sedaka (who was also a recording artist); Burt Bacharach and Hal David; the husband and wife teams of Ellie Greenwich and Jeff Barry, Gerry Goffin and Carole King, and Barry Mann and Cynthia Weil; and many others. (John and Paul's *other* stated ambition—besides becoming "bigger than Elvis"—was to become the "Goffin and King of England.")

The pre-Beatles era in the States was filled with the sounds of surf music, as embodied by the Beach Boys and Jan and Dean, as well as that of girl groups such as the Chiffons and the Shirelles and local acts gone big, such as Philadelphia's Orlons and Dovells. Rock, such as it was, was offered up by such singers as Freddie Cannon and Del Shannon. Dion represented gritty New York street corner crooning, while former gospel singers such as Sam Cooke made a seamless transition into pop. Folk was also quite popular, with the Kingston Trio, the Highwaymen, and Peter, Paul and Mary maintaining a Top 40 presence.

America's record-buying teens had little use for anything coming out of Britain before the Beatles landed. "Telstar," an otherworldly instrumental celebrating a communications satellite, gave the Tornadoes their one and only stateside hit in late 1962, but this was an exception. English-born pop yodeler Frank Ifield reached No. 5 with a World War II-era song, "I Remember You." His presence on the American charts is significant, for his career and the Beatles became intertwined.

As a matter of policy, Capitol Records got first dibs on American rights to any artist signings that their parent company, EMI, was responsible for. They also had the right of refusal if, for whatever reason, they decided that a particular act would be a lost cause in the U.S. market. Before "Love Me Do" was even recorded, Capitol had taken a pass on releasing the Beatles' records, apparently based upon a listen to the Tony Sheridan recordings. To gain a foothold across the ocean, EMI then shopped whom they felt was a surefire smash—Ifield—to Chicago's Vee-Jay Records.

Vee-Jay, specializing largely in R&B acts, was riding high with the success of the Four Seasons. When offered Frank Ifield, who had hit No. 1 in England, they accepted—with the Beatles included in the deal as a "throw-in." Though they passed on "Love Me Do," "Please Please Me" was hard to ignore, and in March 1963 deejay Dick Biondi became the first American to air a Beatles record (though spelled "Beattles" on the label) on WLS, Chicago's high-wattage Top 40 station. The song lasted two weeks and failed to click nationally, but Vee-Jay didn't give up, duly issuing "From Me to You" in May. Unfortunately, the Beatles' version lost out for airplay when going head to head with Del Shannon's concurrent cover. Still, the original made it to No. 116 on the national charts, representing tiny progress.

Despite having the Four Seasons as their primary money-spinner, Vee-Jay was in financial trouble in late summer. The single "She Loves You," which was a mammoth success in Britain, was released stateside not by Vee-Jay but by Philadelphia's Swan Records. The single went largely unnoticed in the U.S. in the fall of 1963, but after a January 1964 reissue it soared to No. 1. The difference in performance can be summed up in two words: Ed Sullivan.

Fab Fact

After headlining a show in England with the Beatles in October 1962, American rocker Little Richard urged concert promoter Don Arden to woo them away from Brian Epstein: "You've got to grab them." Arden declined, though he later managed the career of Beatles copyists ELO (while his daughter Sharon married Ozzie Osbourne).

THE BEATLES CONQUER AMERICA

"I like your advance guard. But don't you think they need haircuts?"
—President Lyndon Johnson to British Prime Minister Sir Alec Douglas-Home, February 12, 1964

In December 1963, just two and a half weeks after devastating news out of Dallas put an end to the New Frontier, producers of the *CBS Evening News* decided that the time was right for a bit of lighthearted froth to close out Walter Cronkite's broadcast. Cronkite ran a clip of the Beatles performing "She Loves You" in Bournemouth, intending to illustrate the novelty of thousands of screaming young English girls and the accompanying fandom.

Among the viewers was fifteen-year-old Marsha Albert, a Silver Springs, Maryland, high school student. What stood out to young Marsha was not the hysteria or the sacks of fan mail depicted, nor the snark of CBS correspondent Alexander Kendrick (who referred to "dishmop" hairstyles and called the group "non-heroes"), but the music. Incensed that her local radio station didn't offer sounds like this, she fired off a letter to deejay Carroll James. As it happened, he too caught the segment, and Marsha's letter stirred him to action.

The WWDC jock arranged to have a friend who worked for BOAC, then a British carrier, fly over a copy of the Beatles' latest single, the newly released "I Want to Hold Your Hand." On December 17, one week after the Cronkite broadcast, he invited Marsha down to the D.C. studio to introduce the record's inaugural spin. What neither one of them knew was that at long last, Capitol, EMI's American outlet, had actually committed to issuing a Beatles record, further backing their agreement with an unprecedented $40,000 promotional push.

Pictured are the Beatles as most Americans met (and remember) them—on Sunday night, February 9, 1964.

Ludwig
THE
BEATLES

ABOVE, LEFT: Washington, D.C., deejay Carroll James, seen here with the Beatles two days after the Sullivan show, forced Capitol's hand by airing "I Want to Hold Your Hand" weeks before the label intended. ABOVE, RIGHT: This twentieth anniversary reissue of "I Want to Hold Your Hand" features one tiny alteration: Paul's offending ciggie has been removed (*see page 52*). Similar censorship befell other images after the 1960s, including the *Abbey Road* sleeve photo. OPPOSITE: The tidal wave that was the Beatles' first American visit proved to be a boon to magazine publishers, who glutted newsstands with fanzines like this "fun kit."

When the Beatles first set foot on New York City soil on February 7, 1964, "I Want to Hold Your Hand" was in its second of seven straight weeks atop the *Billboard* Hot 100 chart, fueling the rapturous reception of screaming girls that greeted them. Two days later, their national television debut on *The Ed Sullivan Show* placed them before 73 million viewers, literally changing lives overnight.

What most believe today to be the kickoff of American Beatlemania was actually the culmination of weeks of behind-the-scenes maneuvering. The story of how this moment arrived represented a perfect storm of circumstance involving a motley array of players, great and small.

Though Ed Sullivan had personally witnessed the adulation of the Beatles back in London, he wasn't immediately sold on booking them. It took a confluence of other factors to bring about what was scarcely the inevitability it seems now. To get things moving, Brian Epstein flew to America in November 1963 with singer Billy J. Kramer in tow. The dual purpose of his visit was to secure cabaret bookings for Kramer while prodding Capitol to finally take up its option on the Beatles.

First, though, Epstein met with Sullivan on November 11 and 12. It so happened that Peter Pritchard, a London-based agent who served as a European talent scout for the Sullivan show, was an acquaintance of Brian's. It was he who first suggested and then arranged the meeting in New York, where Epstein delivered his big pitch. Though the Beatles at that moment still had no record deal in the States (with Vee-Jay in trouble and Swan's release of "She Loves You" being a one-off arrangement), it took all the charm that Epstein could muster to win over the stone-faced TV host.

A few other factors helped. First, Sullivan was aware of the group's recent, highly acclaimed appearance before the Royal Family, which gave him an "angle" to present them. Second, there was the by-now familiar hysteria that accompanied their every public appearance. Also, the "long-haired" look added a layer of novelty. Finally, there was a certain respect for Epstein's negotiating tactics: In exchange for less than the top fee, Sullivan was willing to book the Beatles for *three* straight appearances, top-billing them on the first. (Brian later observed that for the kind of exposure Sullivan's show afforded, *he* would've paid *Ed.*) To Sullivan, their music was simply beside the point.

Next, Epstein contacted Alan Livingston, the president of Capitol Records. "I Want to Hold Your Hand" had had advance orders topping a million in the U.K. Written in response to Brian's request that John and Paul compose something with the American market in mind, they rose to the occasion with this true collaboration, which blended their voices so deftly that they in effect created a *third* voice. The song's shifting dynamics, catchy hook, and exhilarating upward shift ("I want to hold your *h-a-a-a-a-n-d!*") made it a winner. Upon listening to the track over the phone at Brian's insistence, Livingston—who actually hadn't yet heard a note of music from the band, relying instead on his staff—liked what reached his ears. He not only agreed to exercise his option but to support it with an all-out push.

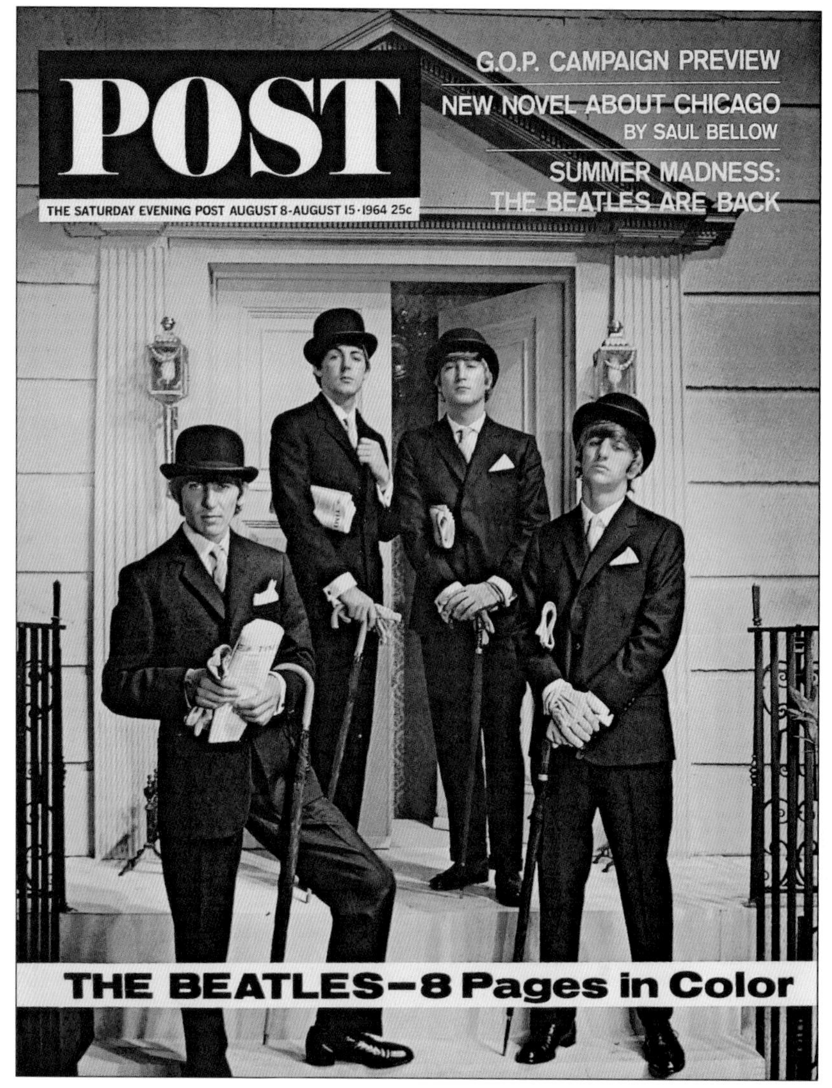

ABOVE: The Beatles' second coming to the New World in August 1964 was splashed across several mainstream magazine covers, including *Life* and *The Saturday Evening Post*. OPPOSITE, TOP: Among the gifts bestowed upon the Beatles during their first visit was an AM-FM transistor radio shaped like a Pepsi machine, shown with George here in *The Beatles: The First U.S. Visit* documentary. OPPOSITE, BOTTOM: Reinforcing his image as the "intellectual Beatle," John published a collection of whimsical drawings and satirical free verse in 1964 as *In His Own Write*. A second volume, *A Spaniard in the Works*, followed in 1965.

That the Beatles were now booked for the Sullivan show was apparently the tipping point. The Capitol brass penciled in January 13, 1964, for issuing the record, giving themselves plenty of time to get their promotion underway. Fate, however, thwarted their well-laid plans. Public demand, stirred by Carroll James (who, in addition to placing the song into heavy rotation on his D.C. station, sent a tape of the record to deejay buddies in Chicago and

St. Louis), dictated otherwise. The label was furious and sent a "cease and desist" letter, but James and his fellow jockeys shrugged it off, citing the will of his listeners. Capitol eventually backed down and, instead, pushed the release date up to December 26.

Meanwhile in England, the Beatles consolidated their grip on the British public. On November 22, *With the Beatles,* their second long-player, hit record store shelves. Contrary to standard American practice, the group issued a *fourteen*-track LP *alongside* a pair of non-album songs (the aforementioned single plus "This Boy" on the B side)—sixteen new recordings in all. Unlike its predecessor, the new album did not have a hit single to hang its success on, but it did contain a number of Lennon-McCartney originals that *could* have been hits, among them "All My Loving" and "It Won't Be Long." George Harrison weighed in with his first original, "Don't Bother Me," while Ringo sang "I Wanna Be Your Man," an original so poorly regarded by its authors that they "gave" it to up-and-comers, the Rolling Stones, for their sophomore single.

The Beatles toured extensively in the U.K. in 1963, beginning the year as a support act but finishing as headliners. As the year came to a close, everything that they had worked so hard for was either realized or within reach: a string of No. 1 singles, a second No. 1 album, sellout concerts, and TV and radio appearances. The one goal left to be attained, success in America, loomed straight ahead.

On the same day that their second album dropped in Britain, CBS television in America ran a short feature on the Beatles during the morning news, filmed days earlier. Plans for an expanded piece to air on Walter Cronkite's evening broadcast that very day were preempted by the assassination of President John F. Kennedy. Instead, it ran on December 10, engaging Marsha Albert and Carroll James and setting events into motion.

It wasn't just CBS that sensed faint rumblings of Beatlemania headed toward America. As the New Year dawned, Jack Paar, the host of NBC's *The Jack Paar Program,* had also heard about the outbreak of mass hysteria across the ocean, and he believed that his viewers would get a kick out of the sight of long-haired rockers and weeping girls. On January 3, 1964, Paar aired a

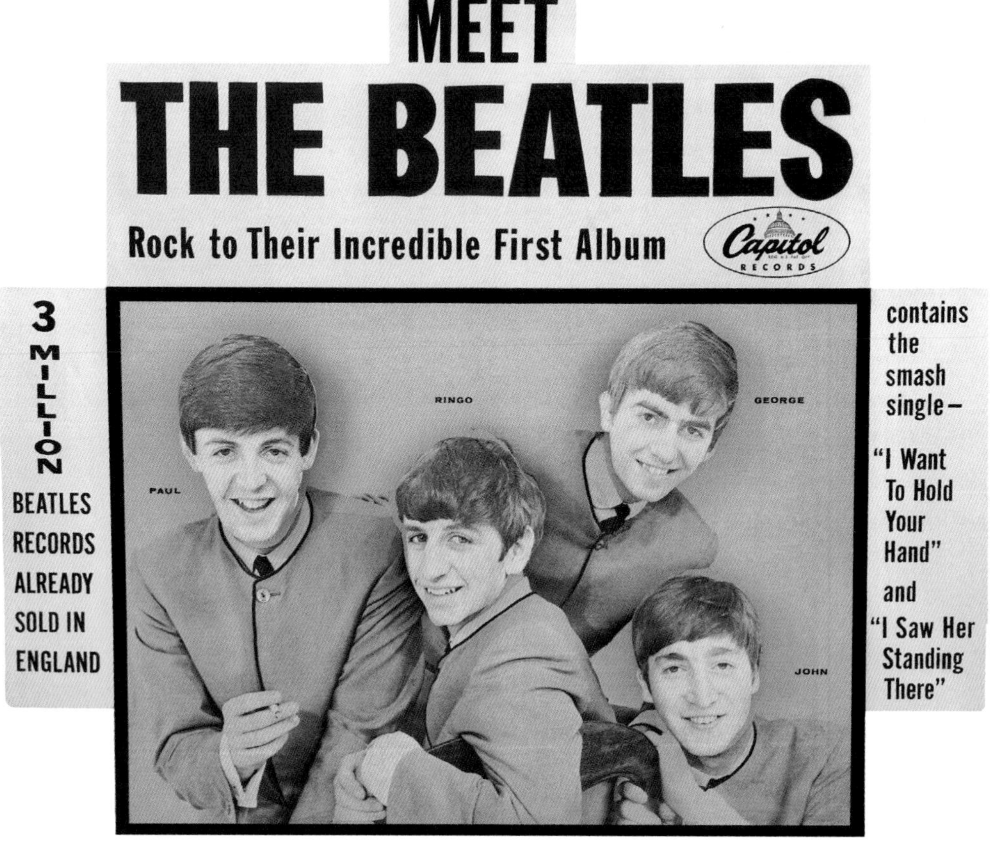

clip of the group, filmed by the BBC. Both Epstein and Sullivan were enraged, the latter feeling that his exclusive had been blown and ordering his aide to cancel the booking. Epstein vented his fury at the BBC for licensing the film, but ultimately cooler heads prevailed. (In fact, Paar *plugged* the upcoming Sullivan appearance.)

Capitol's high-octane promotion fueled Beatlemania. Radio stations across the land were barraged with Beatle wigs, stickers reading "The Beatles are coming," and an open-ended interview disc that allowed local deejays to insert their scripted questions before canned responses from the group, providing the illusion of an actual in-person meeting. For once in the history of promotion, the quality of the product equaled the hype. Though the overall situation hadn't been as tightly controlled as Epstein, Sullivan, and Capitol would have preferred, the end result of their efforts placed the Beatles at the top of the charts at the same time that their TWA jet landed.

ABOVE: Capitol trumpeted the arrival of *Meet the Beatles!* with displays such as this one. The album drew from *With the Beatles* but also included the current single plus *Please Please Me*'s "I Saw her Standing There." OPPOSITE: In addition to the Beatles' "secret diary," the December 1964 issue of *Teen Life* offered stories on several British Invasion acts—plus the Beach Boys.

The screaming that greeted the group on that cold February Friday offered a foretaste of what would become routine that year throughout the world. First impressions were formed as the Beatles met the press at the airport, deftly and wittily answering the sometimes-inane questions they were peppered with:

Q: "Is it true that you're just four English Elvis Presleys?"

Ringo (breaking into a palsied hip-shaking dance): "It's not true! It's not true!"

By the time of the actual broadcast on Sunday night, American interest was reaching a fever pitch. Ed Sullivan, addressing his barely-in-control studio audience, mused that the members of the press bombarding his studio had never seen anything like the excitement surrounding "these four youngsters from Liverpool." After noting that they would be performing in two separate segments, Sullivan wasted no further words: "The Beatles!"

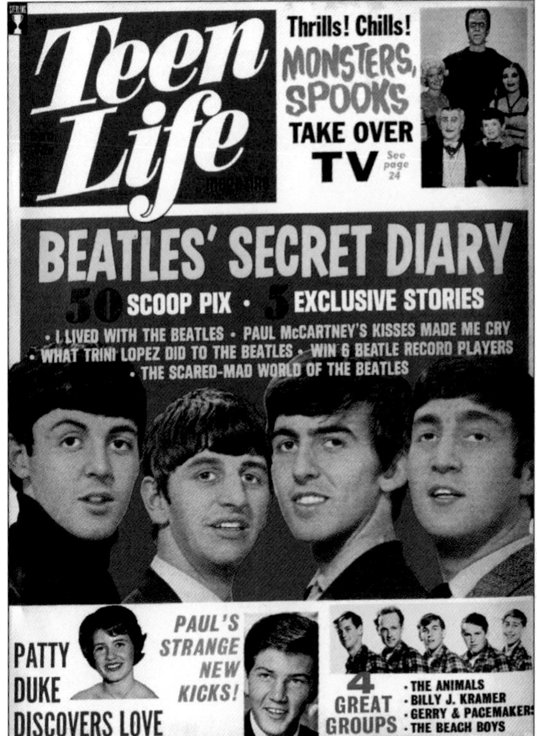

Following Paul's quick count-in, they launched into "All My Loving," an album track from Capitol's *Meet the Beatles!* album, issued two weeks earlier. (Vee-Jay, down but not yet out, released its version of the *Please Please Me* LP, entitled *Introducing...The Beatles,* just ten days before.) The performance stirred plenty of eruptions, such as every time the camera landed on Ringo, or when George joined Paul at the mic. (Their left-handed/right-handed playing styles provided a picturesque symmetry, while at stage left, John's bouncing "wide stance" provided an erotic element for those so inclined.)

Their second song, the pop ballad "Till There Was You," represented a shrewd calculation to win over older viewers. That these long-haired English boys had the good taste to offer up something for everyone was a winning touch, as was the unison bow at the end of the segment, which followed the set-closer "She Loves You." For anyone wondering, the show's director thoughtfully provided onscreen identifications of each Beatle during the second song, carefully noting of John, "Sorry girls—he's married." (This

Fab Fact

The Beatles underwent a rigorous rehearsal and sound check on the afternoon of their first Ed Sullivan Show appearance. However, chalk marks designating microphone levels on the soundboard were later inadvertently wiped by a cleaning lady, resulting in John's vocals being somewhat inaudible during the broadcast.

gesture would be gently parodied years later in the film *That Thing You Do!*) Lest anyone have any doubts, Ed bestowed his blessing upon the foursome. Then, before a final word from Anacin, they were gone.

Though contracted for three straight weeks, the February 9 show represented the *only* time the group was broadcast live from Ed's 57th Street stage. The following week's show was broadcast from Miami, while week three's performance, as well as their 1965 appearances, were broadcast from prerecorded videotape. For 1966, they didn't bother showing up at all, instead sending over film—with a personalized greeting—of "Paperback Writer" and "Rain."

Beyond the Sullivan broadcasts, the Beatles performed a concert in Washington, D.C. The show was aired via closed-circuit broadcast in theaters across the country, affording fans at least the simulation of attending a live show. They also played Carnegie Hall back in New York and logged hours and hours of face time with the media before departing. Even veteran journalists who found it difficult to accept them as anything more than a teenybopper fad found them intelligent, good-humored, and as awed by the attendant phenomenon as anybody else.

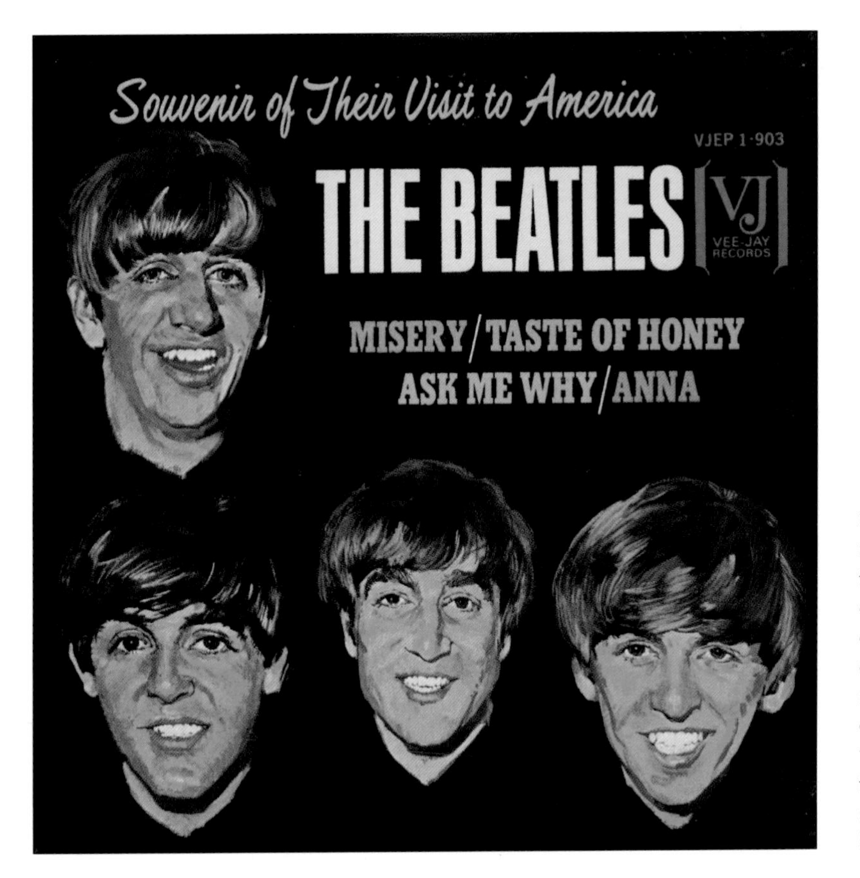

LEFT: Another way Vee-Jay conceived of reselling the same material to fans was to tart it up in new packaging and present it as a "souvenir"—and hope that fans didn't already own the *Introducing the Beatles* album. OPPOSITE and BELOW: Beatles merchandise ran the gamut of all conceivable product: some novel, such as the "official" dolls manufactured by Remco, to the practical, such as the Beatles lunch box (with thermos). Any surviving specimens are highly coveted by Baby Boomers today.

While Epstein did everything right when it came to taking them from a sweaty basement club and putting them on the world stage to be embraced and adored, one area where his vision fell short came with marketing, specifically spin-off products. In 1964, retail outlets across the United States (and indeed, the world) were glutted with all manner of trinkets, toys, magazines, posters, personal care products, clothing, instruments—you name it. Due to their manager's naivety, the Beatles' royalties on the ubiquitous items bearing their name or likeness was just 10 percent in 1964.

At least the Beatles had record sales to sustain them. Once America fell in love with the band, tracks that no one wanted to hear a year previous were suddenly given a re-listen, culminating in a remarkable confluence of chart action in April. During one week, *Billboard's* top five was comprised

"My mother hates them, my father hates them, my teacher hates them. Can you think of three better reasons why I love them?

—Young Beatles fan

ABOVE: Just the chance to catch a glimpse of a Beatle from a distance brought thousands of fans, mostly girls, out to LAX on the eve of their first American tour. OPPOSITE: All talk of rivalries between the Beatles and two of the bands following them to America were largely nonsense. Though the Dave Clark 5 scored several hits initially, their star soon faded, eclipsed by the Rolling Stones and other British imports.

entirely of Beatles releases (on four different labels). On levels no one had ever conceived of, the Beatles were setting records.

The group's success had another, less expected effect: turning Americans into Anglophiles overnight. Suddenly, British acts possessed appeal that a lot of homegrown acts couldn't compete with, as such million-selling artists as Del Shannon and Roy Orbison became virtually passé. Of those following the trail blazed by the Beatles, London's Dave Clark Five arrived first, launching a string of hits throughout 1964 and 1965. Though that quintet was not in the same league as the Beatles artistically, the "Tottenham Sound" was touted as the successor to the "Merseybeat" for at least five minutes.

Somewhat more interesting, at least musically, were the acts that formed Brian Epstein's "stable," among them Gerry and the Pacemakers, Cilla Black, and Billy J. Kramer—Liverpudlians all. Each scored at least one U.S. hit single in the Beatles' wake while benefiting from George Martin's production touch. Although clients of neither Epstein nor Martin, Peter and

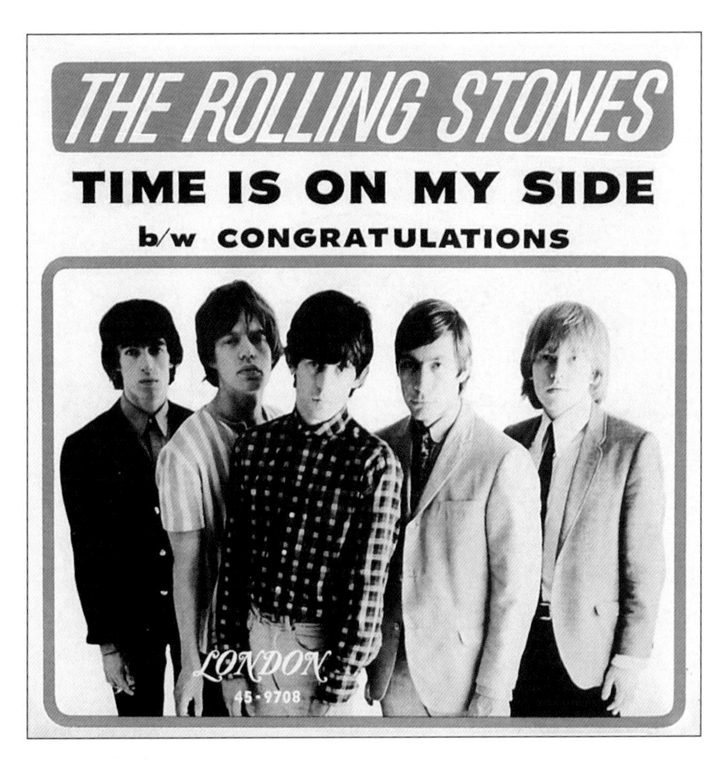

Gordon nonetheless enjoyed several stateside hits through the largesse of the Beatles. Paul McCartney provided the duo with material, beginning with "A World Without Love," which reached No. 1 in June 1964.

Following through the door that the Beatles opened were a host of acts that formed the backbone of what became known as the "British Invasion." Names like the Rolling Stones, the Kinks, the Yardbirds, the Animals, and the Who became familiar to the American record-buying public. Each proved to be much more than a one-hit wonder, and of them, the Stones—after getting a handle on the songwriting thing—became the band that came closest to giving the Beatles any real competition.

The 1964 whirlwind, which saw the Beatles release their first motion picture, *A Hard Day's Night,* and tour the world, resulted in sales of more than 25 million records in the U.S. alone. Topping such unprecedented success would be more than daunting for anyone, but Beatles being Beatles, it wouldn't have occurred to them not to try.

Fab Fact

On August 28, 1964, the Beatles were introduced, as a group, to both Bob Dylan and marijuana. The folkie had assumed that they were already users on the basis of mishearing "I can't hide" as "I get high" in "I Want to Hold Your Hand."

THE WORLD SUCCUMBS

Question: "The French have not made their mind up about the Beatles. What do you think of them?"
Paul: "Oh, WE like the Beatles—they're gear!"

On June 3, 1964, the Beatles convened at a London studio for an early morning photo shoot. Emblematic of the pace of their lives, they were scheduled to squeeze in a recording session later that day on the eve of flying to Copenhagen for the start of their world tour the following day. But their tight schedule was thrown into unexpected disarray when Ringo collapsed, suffering with a 102-degree fever. Doctors diagnosed tonsillitis and called for immediate surgery and rest.

Brian Epstein faced one of his toughest tests yet. Should he cancel the sold-out shows in Denmark, the Netherlands, Hong Kong, New Zealand, and Australia, disappointing thousands of fans in the process, or carry on without their drummer, threatening the group's *esprit de corps?* Good will (and commercial concerns) won out: Upon the recommendation of producer George Martin, Jimmy Nicol (percussionist with the Shubdubs and a studio session pro) was deputized to occupy Ringo's throne until he was fit to rejoin the band.

The bedazzled Nicol was dropped into the machinery literally overnight, barely getting any rehearsal time before being whisked off to a foreign country and the indescribable mania that accompanied virtually every waking Beatles moment. Though easily distinguished from the much-loved drummer he spelled, Nicol received his share of adulation during the week that followed (before Ringo rejoined the band in Melbourne). That the thoroughly professional Nicol would never again enjoy proximity to such stratospheric stardom merely underscored how truly rare the phenomenon that the Beatles generated really was.

John greets beauty pageant contestants on June 8, 1964. The Beatles extended their goodwill to the Far East that month, touring in Hong Kong, New Zealand, and Australia.

3
31
35

Fab Fact

Whenever asked how he was getting along, temporary Beatles drummer Jimmy Nicol always responded, "It's getting better." The laconic phrase became a bit of an inside joke, and years later Paul used it as the foundation for "Getting Better," the fourth track on *Sgt. Pepper.*

Not that they had a moment's rest to reflect upon their singular circumstance. The very night that Nicol entered their lives, the Beatles didn't waste a moment mulling over their drummer's fate; instead, they quietly attended to business, laying down demos for future use: one track destined for Cilla Black (Paul's "It's for You"); another representing George's burgeoning efforts at songwriting ("You Know What to Do"); and the last an effort from John earmarked for their second long-player that year, the sardonically titled *Beatles for Sale* ("No Reply").

The fact that Brian was less concerned with offending his charges than he was the fans lining up around the world to see his "boys" speaks volumes for the care that had gone into launching them as a global act. Knowing the group's fondness for the Hamburg audiences who, after all, helped shape

their destiny, German EMI had the Beatles record German-language versions of "She Loves You" and "I Want to Hold Your Hand" in early 1964. The results were novel but ultimately redundant, as the records were selling quite briskly anyway as originally recorded.

Their universal appeal was fully explicable. The Beatles took American music, filtered it through English sensibilities, wore haircuts inspired by the French, and honed their skills in Germany. (Also, the famed "Beatle boots" they wore featured Cuban heels.) Years later, Paul would declare that if there was any single one message to their collective body of work, it could be summed up in one word: love. What could be more universal?

Left unsaid was that their songs covered an awful lot of ground in that regard, from the adolescent expressions of their early work ("Love Me Do") to more mature thematic explorations ("Norwegian Wood") to romantic trauma ("For No One") to spiritual themes ("Within You Without You") to songs urging self-healing that invited the world to sing along ("Hey Jude"). That everything about them seemed calculated to reach out across cultures was merely their acting upon their native curiosity and natural bent toward

OPPOSITE: Returning to London after a trip to the Netherlands, the Beatles, minus the ailing Ringo, were joined by percussionist Jimmy Nicol, who for a little over a week experienced what only four others ever did: Beatlemania from the inside. ABOVE: Once recovered, Ringo rejoined the group in Australia, no worse for wear.

ABOVE: Some 150,000 fans lined an eight-mile route in July 1964 when the Beatles returned to where it all started, their Liverpool hometown. OPPOSITE: Pictured are some of the unique worldwide issues of Beatles recordings, originating from (*top to bottom*) Peru, Germany, and France.

exploring every avenue of expression open to them. Never before had a rock act conscientiously sought to engage everyone sharing their planet. (Elvis, for instance, never toured the world, despite his legions of fans.)

But all of this was far down the road. Between visits to America in 1964, the Beatles experienced the evidence of their popularity around the world first-hand. In addition to the aforementioned countries, they also visited Sweden (where John and Paul's material existence nearly ended, due to badly grounded electronics at the hockey venue where they were booked) within a full slate of dates in their own homeland.

The English were justifiably proud of the accomplishments "the lads" claimed that year, though, it must be said, there was a bit of a backlash in

Liverpool. Their original fans mourned the "loss" of the group to the outside world, complaining often that the Beatles must have let the adoration go to their heads (rarely did they return home after having long since relocated to London). In fact, after their November appearance at Liverpool's Empire Theatre, they returned just once, a year later.

Winning the world's love was not without cost. It had been a grueling year, with, in addition to touring and recording duties, the added chore of completing a feature film. *A Hard Day's Night* represented success in another medium for the Beatles, who had by this time made their presence ubiquitous on every level. From their premiere on BBC radio in 1962 to their farewell broadcast in June 1965, they had taped eighty-eight songs in nearly three hundred BBC performances. Then, there was the publication of John's humorous drawings and free verse, collected as *John Lennon: In His Own Write.*

Performing light comedy on television became another avenue for extending their exposure. In England, the Beatles had appeared on the *Morecambe and Wise Show,* playing music and cracking wise with the comedy duo. In America, a one-hour special entitled *Around the Beatles* aired in the fall of 1964. The show featured the group performing a short set as well as a spoof of Shakespeare's *A Midsummer Night's Dream.* Also presented were several other acts, including Cilla Black and P. J. Proby, giving priceless stateside exposure to the British singers.

Becoming masters of all media wasn't necessarily Brian Epstein's goal for the group, but they had certainly showed that, given high-quality support, they could acquit themselves well, no matter the setting. An unanticipated byproduct of their popularity was the nonstop clamor for in-person appearances. Clearly, not enough waking hours existed to fulfill every request, but Brian, as usual, was loath to disappoint.

The arrived-at solution was to film the Beatles performing (well, lip-synching) their most recent singles. (Maintaining the illusion of an actual live performance was purely optional.) The film would then be disseminated around the world to whichever television broadcasters wanted to present "The Beatles" on their shows. What are now called "music videos" certainly existed going back as far as the 1940s, if not earlier, but the concept of

"promo films" for TV broadcast in place of a live performance by a popular act was certainly pioneered by, if not definitively invented by, the Beatles.

Topping off a year of goals realized came official validation from the recording industry, which could scarcely ignore the biggest phenomenon of the year, despite their innate conservatism and anti-rock and roll bias. The Beatles were nominated for multiple awards at the Grammys, including Best New Artist and Record of the Year. They won in the first category, beating out English songbird Petula Clark and jazz chanteuse Morgana King. However, "I Want to Hold Your Hand" lost out to Clark's "Downtown" in the Best Rock and Roll Record category. The Grammy marked the beginning of many such establishment awards, though their losing out to the Anita Kerr Singers the following year for Best Vocal Group Performance has become widely seen as proof of the industry's cluelessness.

As 1965 dawned, the Beatles found themselves on a schedule similar to the previous year's: recording; another film to make; another book from John (*A Spaniard in the Works*); more recording; and touring. This time, the film was in color (*Help!*) and the dates were Continental: France, Italy, and Spain. Language proved no barrier to the thousands of fans who turned out, not just for the shows but to greet the Beatles at the airport. Sometimes fans lined the streets all the way to the hotel.

Though the Beatles generally found their receptions around the globe to be grandiose, there was one corner of the world that was slightly less impressed with them. A Peking (now Beijing), China, newspaper called the group "monsters," asserting that they produced "an unpleasant noise to satisfy the Western world's need for crazy and rotten music." (The same article forecast the demise of Great Britain, so it's possible that their assessment may have been slightly biased.)

But on the whole, 1965 saw the group fully established as superstars. They had reached the top of the ladder, and their triumphs were becoming practically routine. Breaking the established pattern was some rather unexpected news out of Buckingham Palace: In June, the Beatles became Members of the Most Honorable Order of the British Empire (MBE). Though it was rather a low rank in the scheme of such honors, knighthood being at the

ABOVE: No matter where in the world the Beatles appeared (France, in this instance), fan reaction was universal. OPPOSITE: This German EP sleeve depicts the Beatles on Salisbury Plain near Stonehenge, as seen in *Help!*

top, it was also the first time anyone in their profession had been so recognized.

While the Beatles took the notice in stride (as something more than another gold record), some previous recipients were outraged, feeling that the award (which included a medal and investiture by the Queen herself) had been irrevocably debased. At least a dozen "gongs" were returned in protest, but John, increasingly defining himself as the group's most outspoken member, merely noted that most of the protesters had received theirs for military service: "...for killing people. We got ours for entertaining. I'd say we deserve ours more."

Though the Beatles were never so casual as to actually wear their medals in public, they did don them for the *Sgt. Pepper* cover shoot two years later.

AMERICAN FANDOM

"I'd look over at John and say, 'Christ, look at you; you're a bloody phenomenon!' and just laugh...'cause it was only him, you know."
—Ringo

New York City theatrical promoter Sid Bernstein had built quite a successful career with such artists as Judy Garland and Tony Bennett among his clientele. But he was also an Anglophile, having acquired a taste for British culture while serving overseas during World War II. He kept up with events across the sea via weekly deliveries of English newspapers, and in the fall of 1963 his astute radar made him among the first in America to become aware of the burgeoning phenomenon of Beatlemania.

Recognizing what a coup it would be to book the act in New York (while having heard not a note of their music), Bernstein placed a long-distance call to Brian Epstein after reading in *Variety* that the Beatles were coming in February to do the Sullivan show. Epstein, well aware that at that moment his charges had yet to score an American hit of any kind, resisted the entreaty until Bernstein pledged to get them into the prestigious Carnegie Hall. Now *that* was exactly the right card to play with Epstein, who more than anything craved respect and validation from the establishment.

Shrewdly, Bernstein booked the group for February 12—Lincoln's birthday and, therefore, a school holiday—virtually guaranteeing to a skeptical Epstein that the two shows would sell out. His instincts proved correct, and with this bit of success, he was ready to make his big pitch to the Beatles' manager. Epstein, now impressed, listened to Bernstein's grandiose plan to book them the following year at a *baseball stadium,* something unheard of for a rock band. Again, Brian—fearing that the sight of the boys playing before a half-empty venue would be a humiliation impossible to live down—refused to entertain the offer without first seeing some cash up front: $50,000, to be precise.

The tens of thousands of fans attending the Shea Stadium concert were hardly able to hear the Beatles over the sound of their own adoration. Some got so carried away that they climbed the netting behind home plate.

But Bernstein knew the market by this time, and strictly by word of mouth he managed to sell out the newly built Shea Stadium, home of the New York Mets. The Beatles were booked at the ballpark for Sunday, August 15, 1965, a day after taping a performance to air on *The Ed Sullivan Show* four weeks later. The show would kick off their second U.S. tour, one that saw them perform in half as many cities as the year before—not because of any diminished popularity, but because the 1964 twenty-five city jaunt had been so grueling. This time out, they would play ten cities but in bigger venues, and typically two shows a day.

The Beatles' first Shea Stadium concert represented the high-water mark of Beatlemania. With the band largely unhindered by any real controversy to this point, the show, before 55,000 fans, demonstrated for any lingering skeptics that they were no passing fancy. They had arrived, their success was no fluke, and there was no doubting that they had tapped into something within youth culture that would blossom as the decade unfolded. Elvis at his greatest success had never influenced the changes in entertainment, fashion, and the thinking of an entire generation the way the foursome from Liverpool had.

Fab Fact

Sixteen-year-old Meryl Streep was in attendance on that sultry Sunday evening at Shea. So were two future Beatles wives: Linda Eastman and Barbara Bach (nee Goldbach), who was not yet a fan; she was merely chaperoning her younger sister.

Shea represented the face of American fandom. Though the Beatles drew huge crowds no matter where they went, everything was always bigger, splashier, and louder in the U.S. If the group released one album and one single in Britain, in the States it somehow translated into *two* albums that the Beatles themselves were hard-pressed to keep track of. (John struggled at Shea with remembering how their material had been marketed. When introducing "Baby's in Black" as coming from "one of those albums," he finally conceded that he was unsure exactly which one: "I haven't got it.")

It was Beatlemania on steroids, as the group's image was splashed across dozens of newsstand publications. The Beatles' sound dominated every

OPPOSITE: Maybe it was the August heat, maybe it was so many bodies crammed together, or maybe it was an overload of excitement from seeing the Beatles in the flesh, but the Shea Stadium concert did take its toll on some. BELOW: The day before the Shea show, the Beatles taped an appearance on *The Ed Sullivan Show* for broadcast the following month (*pictured*). Ed returned the favor by introducing them on the Shea stage.

ABOVE: John distinguished himself on the Sullivan broadcast with his inability to remember the words to their current single, "Help!" OPPOSITE, TOP: Just as 1964 had been the year of the Beatles, 1965 saw the Rolling Stones at last capture a sizable stateside following, bolstered by the success of "(I Can't Get No) Satisfaction," which they wrote and recorded while on tour in America. OPPOSITE, BOTTOM: As noted on the cover of *16's Spectacular*, the Beatles met Elvis—on August 27, 1965, in Bel Air, California. Though much anticipated, the evening proved to be a rather low-key affair as the musicians sat around and jammed.

Top 40 radio station, and "long hair," once a reference to venerable classical composers, became shorthand for anything youth, British, or Beatles related.

Old-school comedians could don a Beatles wig and get a laugh, while anything deemed Beatles approved would suddenly become a new craze. (An early manifestation of this came when George off-handedly mentioned in a 1963 interview a fondness for "jelly babies," an English candy. In America, this translated to "jelly beans," a much harder confection, and the Beatles found themselves pelted with the tiny missiles by well-meaning fans who didn't know any other way to express their devotion.)

Well before their second full-scale American tour began, the British Invasion that the Beatles had spearheaded a year earlier had taken root in the former colony. In 1964, eighteen singles from English acts landed in *Billboard*'s Top 100 of the year, not including an additional nine from the Beatles themselves. In 1965, the number of British singles rose to twenty-five, not including the Fab Four's. (By comparison, in 1963—before the

Beatles landed—there were exactly none.) Though several of the artists fell by the wayside over time (Chad and Jeremy; the Honeycombs; Freddie and the Dreamers), others emerged that would give the Beatles a run for their money in the years to come, none more so than the Rolling Stones.

The Stones' American success in 1965—with "(I Can't Get No) Satisfaction" topping the year's best-selling singles—represented a triumph of artistry *and* marketing, pitting the Stones' yin against the Beatles' yang. Whereas the latter group wanted to hold your hand, the former was more direct, declaring (by way of Willie Dixon) "I just want to make love to you." The Stones' manager, Andrew Oldham, cannily played off the Beatles' clean-cut image by presenting his clients as the bad boy alternative. In the same year that saw one group honored by the Queen while the other was fined for urinating on a gas station wall, Oldham didn't really have to work all that hard.

The reality was that, for all their posturing, the Stones shared a lot with their better-known counterparts and were profoundly influenced by them. After the Beatles released a string-laden ballad, "Yesterday," in a departure from their usual sound, the Rolling Stones recorded "As Tears Go By." After the Beatles brought the exotic-sounding Indian sitar into the studio to record "Norwegian Wood," the Stones responded with "Paint It Black" the following year. Though relations were quite friendly between the bands, there was also an undeniable undercurrent of competition. Both groups, recognizing their status, took care to avoid actual head-to-head competition in the charts by alternating release dates, lest they compromise each others' sales.

The Beatles' musical influence was certainly felt across the pond as well. Two of the biggest peer acts in America were of Southern California origin. The Beach Boys of Hawthorne, California, were a five-man ensemble that specialized in close harmonies and Chuck Berry recyclings, at least initially. But their creative leader, Brian Wilson, was a profoundly musical soul whose ambitions could not be fully expressed within the limitations of hot rod anthems and surfing ditties. From the start, there was an undercurrent of introspection evident in compositions such as "In My Room" and "Warmth of the Sun" that belied their apparent frat boy leanings (embodied by front

"I started mixing up old folk songs with the Beatles beat and taking them down to Greenwich Village and playing them for the people there."

—Roger McGuinn of the Byrds

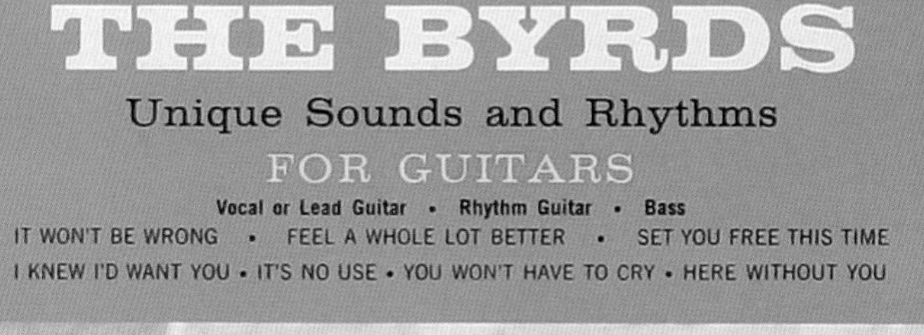

man Mike Love). But Wilson was quick to recognize that the Beatles represented a challenge to extend his musical boundaries into uncharted waters.

The other Los Angeles-area act to be affected by the Fab Four in a profound way began its recording career first as the Jet Set and then, in honor of the colorfully garbed guards outside Buckingham Palace, the Beefeaters. Fronted by Jim (later known as Roger) McGuinn, the Byrds started out firmly aboard the folk bandwagon. But two events—the Beatles' *Ed Sullivan Show* appearance and later their film *A Hard Day's Night*—proved literally life changing. The first offered an epiphany to the folkies: that drawing ostentatious devotion from prepubescent girls didn't preclude the possibility of talent. "[The Beatles] put together the rockabilly scene...they mixed it with blues and bossa nova and classical and all kinds of influences," recalled McGuinn. "It was tremendously appealing to someone who had been in folk music.... I went 'Ah! This is really cool.'"

The Beatles' big-screen debut just months later had the effect of handing the nascent rockers a road map. McGuinn reported that when *A Hard Day's Night* arrived in theaters, he and his fellow future Byrds (the band included David Crosby and Gene Clark) went to see it the same way an anthropologist in the field studies an alien culture. What he saw floored him: George Harrison was getting those distinctive ringing tones from a Rickenbacker *twelve-string electric guitar.* Thus it was that the Byrds' signature sound on such hits as "Mr. Tambourine Man" and "Turn! Turn! Turn!" came from seeing—and hearing—a singular instrument depicted throughout the Beatles' first film.

But influences were always a two-way street with the Fabs. Though their success profoundly impacted many rock bands on both sides of the ocean, they never ceased being receptive themselves. A musician who profoundly shaped their artistic direction—and indeed that of any one of their peers who aspired to offering something beyond mere entertainment—was the inscrutable bard from Hibbing, Minnesota, Bob Dylan.

Born Robert Zimmerman, Dylan started his musical career sharing the same Buddy Holly/Little Richard fixations that the Beatles did, but his earliest public persona was as an earnest Woody Guthrie disciple in New York's Greenwich Village. With such songs as "A Hard Rain's A-Gonna Fall" and "Blowing in the Wind," Dylan was in his own way laying the groundwork for something new in rock. Fusing lyrics rich in metaphor with personal poetry was virtually unheard of in the Top 40.

It therefore seemed to the public that the Beatles and Dylan occupied wholly separate worlds. But by the end of 1964, it became clear that a distinct Dylan influence was creeping into the group's usually sunny music.

OPPOSITE: The Byrds themselves might have used the very words shown on this chord book to describe their music: "unique sounds and rhythms." ABOVE, TOP: Ringo's distinction as the group's resident Countrypolitan was demonstrated with his performance of the Buck Owens hit "Act Naturally" on their Ed Sullivan appearance in 1965. ABOVE, BOTTOM: The Beach Boys' infatuation with the Beatles was made explicit on their all-covers album, *Beach Boys' Party!* The 1965 release contained no less than *three* Lennon-McCartney originals.

Bob Dylan and the Beatles maintained a two-way infatuation. As Dylan "went electric," expanding his fan base while alienating folk purists with *Bringing It All Back Home,* the Beatles' musical maturity, inspired by Dylan's sophistication, increased discernibly. The lightweight pop and roll featured on *Beatles VI* gave way to more philosophical offerings such as "We Can Work It Out" by year's end.

On *Beatles for Sale,* John's "I'm a Loser" bore more than a little hint of Dylan's self-reflective bent, complete with a harmonica solo that sounded nothing like the group's earliest singles. Other traces were equally clear, such as on *Help!*'s "You've Got to Hide Your Love Away," which incorporated Dylan-esque imagery ("feeling two foot small") to convey the singer's alienation. Through Dylan's influence, the Beatles broadened their emotional palette and sang about issues that transcended the standard Tin Pan Alley traditions that most of their peers studiously adhered to.

As for Dylan, when he had first heard "I Want to Hold Your Hand" on the radio, rather than sneer at the puerile sentiments expressed in a song that had been embraced by the least sophisticated segment of the public, he picked up on something fundamental that escaped most listeners' attention. "They were doing things nobody was doing," he observed. "Their chords were outrageous, just outrageous, and their harmonies made it all valid. Everybody else thought they were...gonna pass right away. But it was obvious to me that they had staying power. I knew they were pointing the direction of where music had to go."

Exactly where music was going was anyone's guess in 1964–65, but for

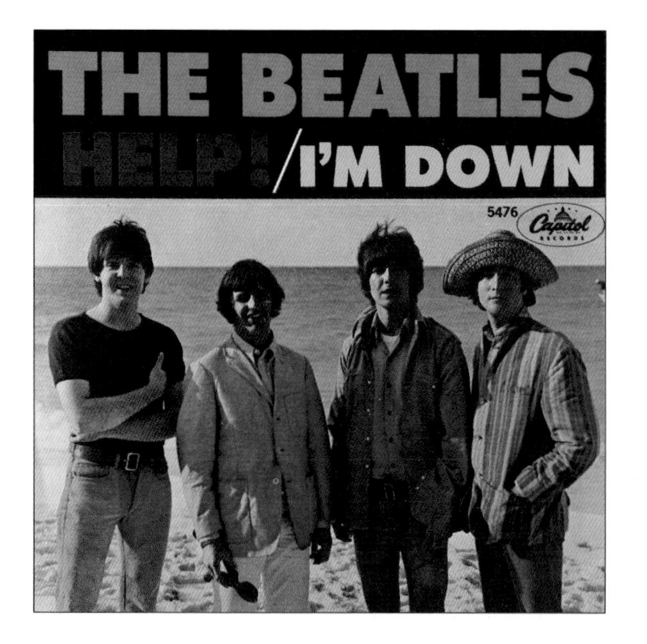

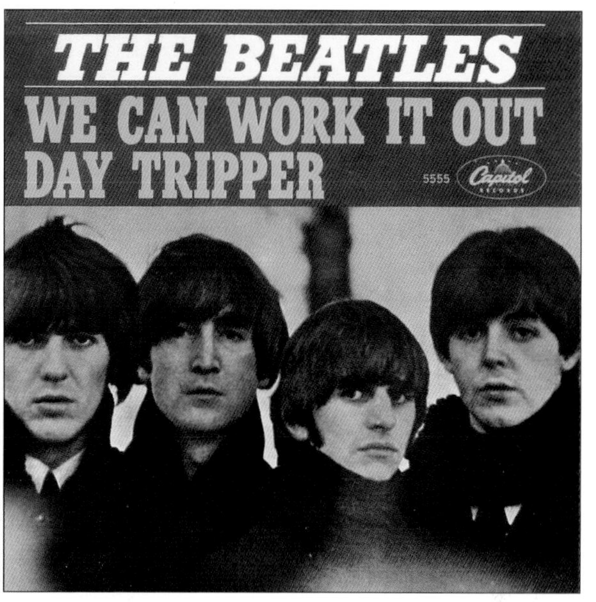

the Beatles the one constant was increased sophistication coupled with chart success. Singles released in America in 1965 included "Eight Days a Week," "Ticket To Ride," "Help!," and "Day Tripper," which was backed with "We Can Work It Out." Each new single marked an advance in both the Lennon-McCartney songwriting team and the foursome's stretching of the beat group paradigm.

Though open-mindedness was a hallmark of their sound, the band wasn't always immediately comfortable with untested waters. "Yesterday" was a case in point. The bittersweet ballad that the world knows and loves today (it is the most covered song ever, with more than 3,000 versions) started out as a melody that came to Paul as he slept. Upon waking, he quickly found the chords on the piano beside his bed, but the words were slow in coming. For months, he walked around singing, "Scrambled eggs/Oh my baby, how I love your legs." When the time at last came to record the song, George Martin's mind's ear heard an arrangement that augmented the composer's simple acoustic guitar part with a string quartet—and nothing more. Not only was a solo performance in every sense being issued under the group brand, but it also bore the trappings of a sound far removed from their rock and roll

"Rubber Soul blew my mind.... It sounds like a collection of songs that belong together, and it was an uplifting feeling. So I thought I'd make a collection of songs—called Pet Sounds."

—Brian Wilson of the Beach Boys, whose *Pet Sounds* was ranked as the second greatest album of all time (behind *Sgt. Pepper*) by *Rolling Stone*

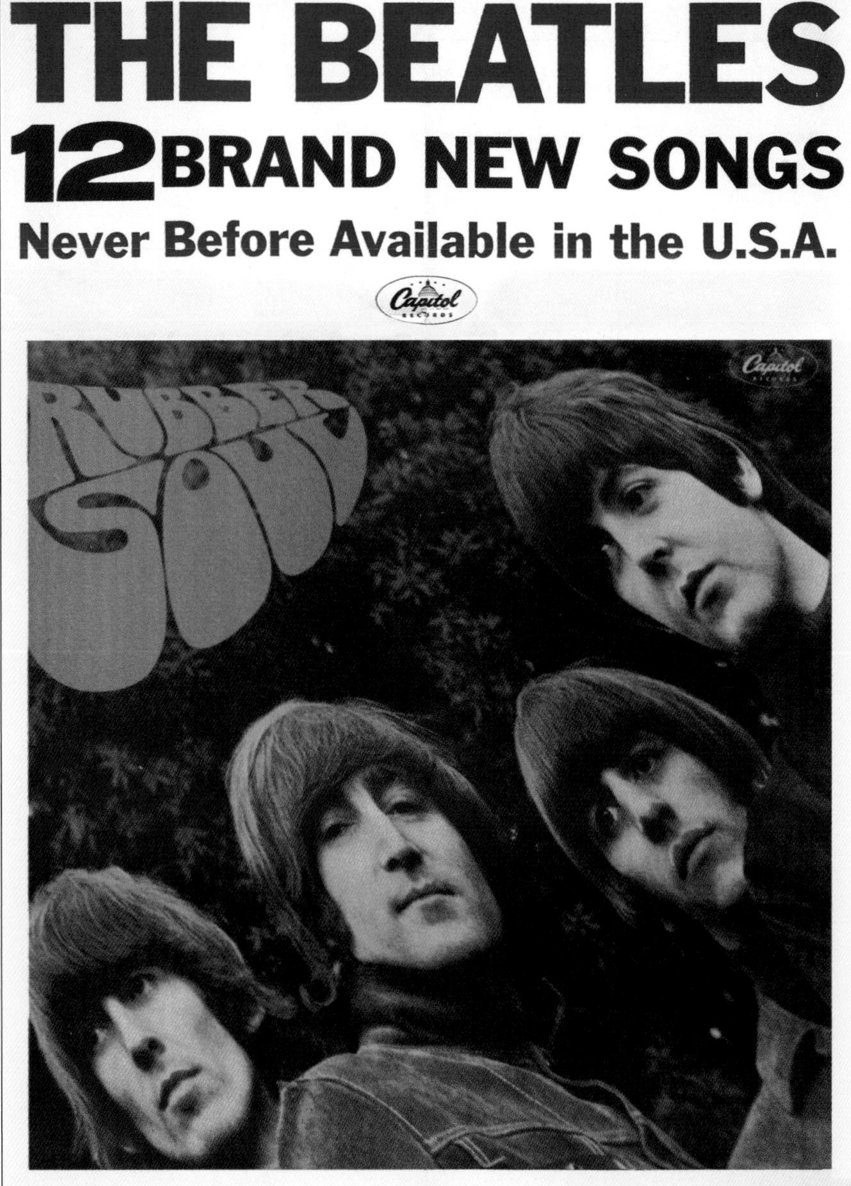

roots.

Though the final results were recognized as something special, the Beatles were also well aware of what a departure "Yesterday" was from what fans had come to expect from them. As such, they fought the pressure from their record label to release it as a group single, at least in England. In America, where Capitol operated fairly unfettered by this time, the song did see issue, whereupon it shot to the top of the charts. It stayed there for a month until displaced by the Rolling Stones' "Get Off of My Cloud."

"Yesterday" was plugged on the Beatles' September 12th *Ed Sullivan Show* appearance, but not on their summer American tour. What was becoming increasingly evident was the divergence between what the Beatles were laying onto vinyl and what they were capable of pulling off onstage. While gamely playing stadiums utterly unsuited for allowing the musicians to hear themselves above the screaming adoration of fans, it was equally clear that such shows were mere spectacle, with no real chance for a nuanced composition to successfully come across under such chaotic conditions. The Beatles by this time saw themselves as wearing two hats: the crowd-pleasing entertainers cranking out their greatest hits in concert by rote, and the serious artists who made increasing use of the recording studios' capabilities. For the time being at least, satisfying both demands was all in a day's work.

The year ended with the release of *Rubber Soul,* a major leap forward as the Beatles distilled their Dylan influence with that of Motown funk and Byrdsian folk rock. Tunes such as Paul's "I'm Looking Through You," John's "In My Life," and George's "If I Needed Someone" showed thoughtful listeners that their days of playing baseball parks were numbered. Meanwhile, their legions of fans continued to support their artistic growth by making every new product a bestseller.

Perhaps the most amazing aspect of these two years of nonstop activity was that, despite all of the demands made on them—films, television and radio appearances, concerts, interviews, and so forth—the Beatles not only got better and better at what they did, but they managed to retain their sanity.

No small accomplishment.

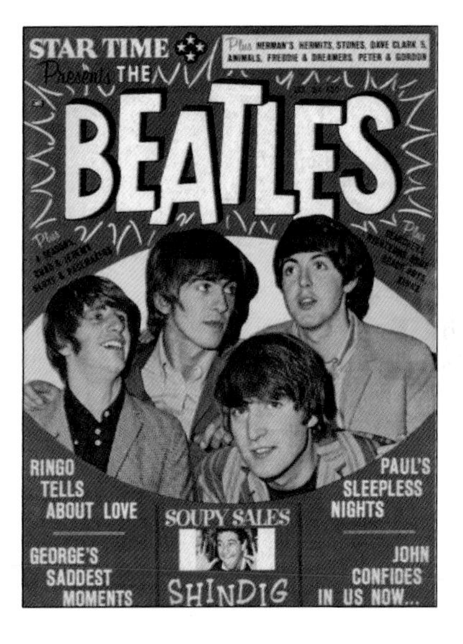

OPPOSITE: Released at Christmas in 1965, Capitol's reconception of *Rubber Soul* actually worked as a cohesive *au courant* folk/rock-flavored album. ABOVE: Despite their obvious artistic growth, the Beatles remained a popular subject for standard issue teen tabloids, such as *Star Time* magazine.

THE FAB FOUR ON FILM

"I think because I loved films, I was less embarrassed than the others to be in one.... I felt a lot of the time that George didn't want to be there."—Ringo

"I don't know what he's talking about. I loved it!"—George

The increasing hysteria generated by the Beatles in late 1963 did not escape the notice of those whose livelihood it was to spot the next big thing (and get a lock on it). For London-based film executive Bud Orenstein, in the employ of United Artists, the mass adulation over a pop group meant one thing: a lot of *soundtrack recordings* could be sold. Orenstein was not certain that the Beatles' thespian skills would be enough to carry a successful picture. But he and UA producer Walter Shenson concluded that no matter the *film*'s fate, UA could make back a healthy return on its investment simply by having the soundtrack album issued through the studio's record division. (EMI's foresight in signing the group did not extend to recordings done for film.)

In negotiating the deal, Brian Epstein again showed that his business acumen was as woeful with the film industry as it was with merchandising. Meeting in October 1963 with Orenstein and Shenson, he agreed to a deal for a low-budget "exploitation" picture—after all, if the Beatles were sincere in their aim to outshine Elvis, they could hardly ignore the King's cinematic efforts (such as they were). But Epstein told the two men in no uncertain terms that he could not accept anything less than a 7.5 percent share of the film's profits. No problem; they had been prepared to offer 25 percent.

Enrichment missteps aside, both the Beatles and Brian were adamant about one thing: Though recognizing that United Artists wanted to push the project into production quickly—before their star faded—they demanded a quality writer and director. For the latter, Shenson was quick to oblige

Pattie Boyd takes a comb to her future husband's famous locks on the set of *A Hard Day's Night*. The other girls are (*left to right*) Tina Williams; Pru Bury, who played "Rita" to Pattie's "Jean"; and Susan Whitman.

George Harrison
Ringo Starr
Paul McCartney
John Lennon

them. American expatriate Richard Lester had carved a successful career for himself in London, directing television shows, commercials, and low-budget films. Though not exactly a "big name," Lester did possess the virtue of knowing how to shoot music *and* comedy, having directed *It's Trad, Dad!*—a starring vehicle for Helen Shapiro.

The Beatles and Lester hit it off immediately, sharing a common love of absurdist humor. (Like George Martin, Lester impressed the group with his past work with The Goons.) Finding the ideal writer was slightly trickier, but a Welsh-born, Liverpool-raised television playwright named Alun Owen proved an inspired choice. Owen had an ear for natural-sounding dialogue, possessed well-honed observational skills, and had a grasp of the native Scouser wit.

Owen spent several days traveling with the band to Sweden in late October. What he came away with formed the basis of their first feature film, originally (and rather unimaginatively) titled *Beatlemania* before a Ringo-ism (as retold by John) supplanted it: *A Hard Day's Night.* First, Owen depicted the foursome as prisoners of their fame, spending their waking hours constantly being shuttled from a car to a gig to another car to a hotel and so

ABOVE: The claims made of a "hilarious, action-packed" film in this poster for *A Hard Day's Night* were echoed by audiences and critics. LEFT: Director Richard Lester, shown with Ringo in the documentary *You Can't Do That: The Making of A Hard Day's Night,* made good use of his unschooled actors by playing to their strengths as personalities. OPPOSITE: Lester's knack for surreal images was evident throughout the film, including this scene in which George schools "Shake" (actor John Junkin) in the use of a safety razor.

forth, completely isolated from interacting with anyone but their handlers. Second, his shorthand impressions of the four personalities took hold as stereotypes for the remainder of their existences: John, the witty iconoclast and resident subversive; Paul, the crowd-pleasing charmer; George, the laconic deadpan; and Ringo, the sad-faced urchin in need of mothering.

Though each characterization contained a kernel of truth, the Beatles themselves would express varying degrees of distaste for being typed thusly. Still, it provided a large segment of the population—those not given to nuance—a handle for distinguishing each Beatle. (Comparisons to the Marx Brothers abounded, but those comparisons rankled some, Groucho Marx included. He spoke for many of the old guard when he groused that he couldn't tell *any* of the four Liverpudlians apart.)

Filmed in black and white for a half-million dollars, *A Hard Day's Night* had the look of a documentary, albeit a frenetic and, at times, surreal one. It was built around the improbability of a live TV broadcast coming off without a hitch, owing to complications instilled by the presence of Paul's fictitious grandfather. He was played to droll perfection by television actor Wilfrid Brambell, a familiar fixture to Brits for his role on the comedy *Steptoe and Son*

Fab Fact

Both A *Hard Day's Night* and *Help!* featured sequences deleted from the final release, including an extended Paul solo scene in the first film. When Richard Lester visited the United Artists film vault in the early 1970s to re-screen the unused footage, he discovered to his eternal regret that the studio had summarily disposed of it, per standard practice, after five years.

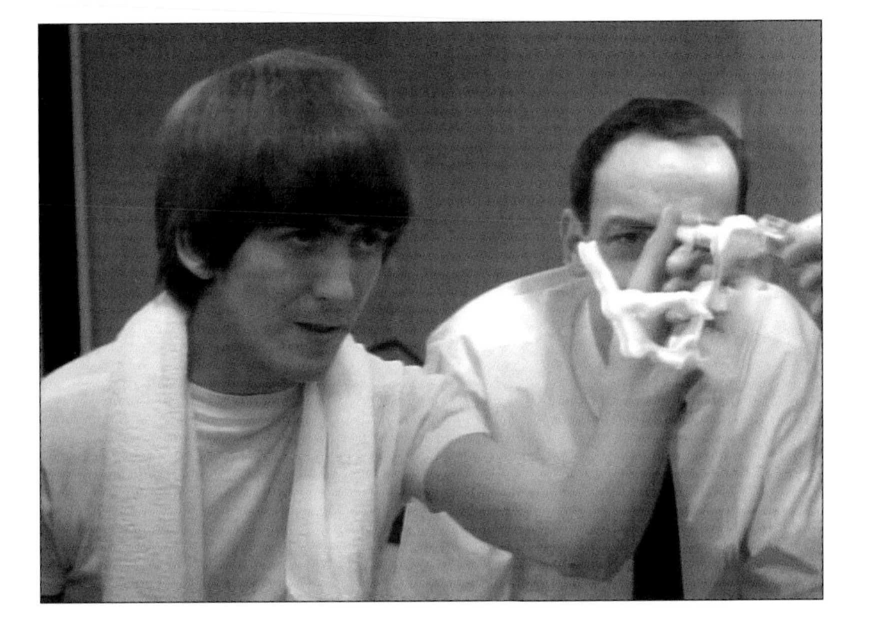

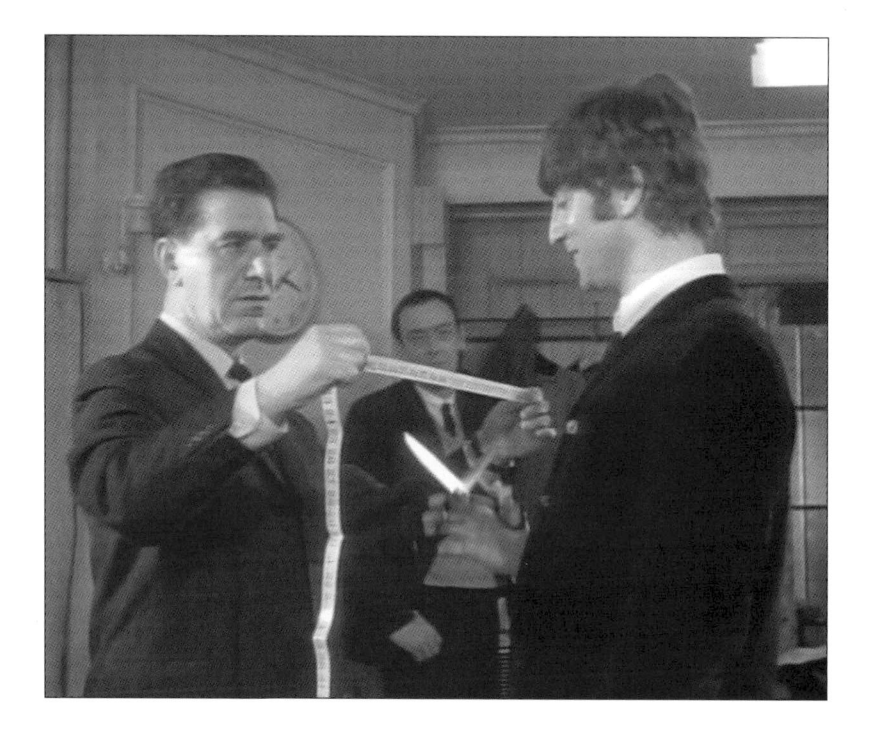

(remade in the U.S. as *Sanford and Son*). The senior "McCartney" was placed in his grandson's custody to give him a change of scenery after a romantic disappointment, but the elderly gentleman (in reality, Brambell was fifty-two) instead stirred up trouble for the sheer pleasure of it at every turn.

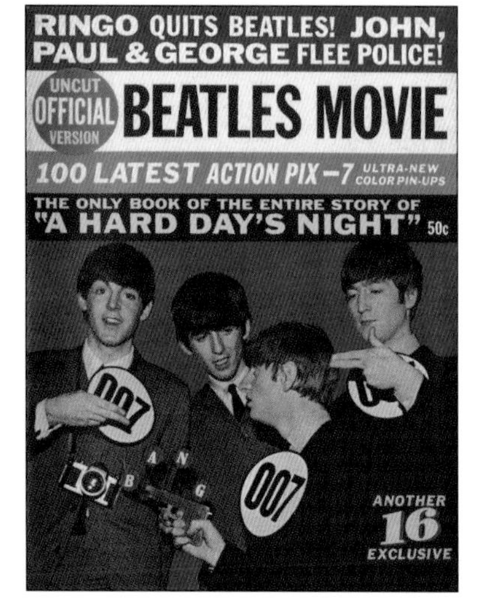

Like the very records the Beatles were making, the film projected exuberance and fun, being a stylish blend of dry wit and technical innovation. Indeed, director Lester's groundbreaking use of jump cuts, hand-held cameras, unusual angles, and vari-speed created a virtual blueprint for future rock music videos—something that MTV felt compelled to honor him for one day (but a title Lester was loath to accept). Critics expecting little from what was anticipated as another quickie cash-in were instead charmed by both the film craft and the Beatles themselves, which resulted in what film critic Andrew Sarris described as "the *Citizen Kane* of jukebox musicals." The film grossed more than $6 million in the U.S. alone, making it a brilliant success on every level.

Cited for special notice was Ringo. Each Beatle was accorded a solo scene (although Paul's ended up on the cutting room floor), but the drummer's scene proved the most memorable. Gone off "parading"—out on strike—at the instigation of Paul's grandfather, a heavily hung over Ringo was given a platform for enacting an homage to Lester's silent film comic heroes, loaded with sight gags and pathos. As the bittersweet tones of "This Boy" (rechristened "Ringo's Theme") played, he was shown as adrift at sea in the cold world without the support of his mates. It was a perception that most took at face value even outside the film.

Naturally, their next movie would build upon the success of the first. The same producer/director team was used, as were other actors who had appeared in the earlier film. One, Victor Spinetti, had developed quite a rapport with the Beatles. From his role as the neurotic TV director in the first film, he segued into a high-strung mad scientist in the second. (He would later make a cameo in *Magical Mystery Tour.*) The budget was tripled, partly due to filming in color and also due to filming in exotic locales, including the Bahamas and the Austrian Alps. (Having learned a lesson or two since *A Hard Day's Night,* Brian pushed for the Bahamas in part as a tax dodge.)

Filming began in February 1965 on *Help!,* which was originally titled *Eight Arms to Hold You*—a reference not to the four Beatles but to the statue of the Eastern goddess, Kali, seen throughout. Since the team was determined not to make *A Hard Day's Night II,* this time the plot went all out in the opposite direction. Instead of the first film's hyperrealism, *Help!* was a virtual live-action cartoon, presenting the boys as recipients of unwanted attention—not from screaming girls, but from a thuggish Far East religious cult as well as an inept duo bent on ruling the world. Lester deftly blended a satire on the then-current James Bond vogue with the over-the-top campiness that TV's *Batman* would explore more fully the following year.

As such, it may have succeeded *too* well. The film alienated some critics as well as the Beatles themselves, who had trouble wrapping their minds around the concept. The heightened profile of their supporting cast had the effect of making the Beatles feel like guests in their own film. But the benefit of hindsight reveals the film's charms. To begin with, *Help!*'s musical numbers (with one exception) went even further into the realm of fantasy,

Fab Fact

Wilfrid Brambell (*pictured*) and Ringo came very close to an onscreen reunion in Frank Zappa's 1971 project, *200 Motels.* After several days on the set, Brambell stormed out of the project, outraged at the film's more salacious aspects. He was replaced by Ringo's chauffeur.

OPPOSITE, TOP: Cast as a costumer in *A Hard Day's Night* was the Beatles' real-life tailor, Dougie Millings, who designed their famous collarless suits. OPPOSITE, BOTTOM: Though the Beatles are shown spoofing the James Bond craze on the cover of this *16* special, not until *Help!* did Dick Lester attempt an actual onscreen 007 send-up.

functioning as self-contained musical videos dropped in as visual segues from scene to scene.

"It was like having clams in a movie about frogs."

—John, on *Help!*

The "Ticket to Ride" sequence is especially memorable. Documenting the group on skis for the first time, Lester captured their youthful exuberance for possibly the last time amidst their tumbles and cutting up. (George Martin, along for the ride but not really on duty, distinguished himself off-camera by breaking his ankle on the slopes during the filming.) Lester also displayed a serendipitous touch: When a string of power lines threatened to ruin his shot, he simply turned the wires into a musical staff, superimposing the appropriate notes onto them.

Ringo was front and center as wearer of the coveted and apparently irremovable sacrificial ring. This necessarily diminished his fellows, but with a soundtrack featuring the title cut, "Ticket to Ride," "You've Got to Hide Your Love Away," and "You're Gonna Lose That Girl"—all John compositions, as it happened—the Beatles as a musical force were certainly depicted at the top of their game.

Also, *Help!* tended to grow on one with repeated viewings. True, it didn't have the freshness and immediacy of its predecessor, but it did feature colorful characters such as Leo McKern (of *Rumpole of the Bailey* fame) as Clang and Roy Kinnear, who would later play the father of Veruca Salt in *Willy Wonka & the Chocolate Factory*. For the Beatles, work on the film proved a good opportunity to visit vacation spots while indulging in copious amounts of marijuana—so much so that filming had to be stopped during numerous takes during which they collapsed in fits of giggles.

Their deal with United Artists called for three motion pictures, but a worthwhile third script proved elusive. Instead, 1966 saw John Lennon acting in a non-Beatles role in Richard Lester's black comedy *How I Won the War*. Having retired from touring, John was at loose ends and readily took up the director's invitation. Though the role of musketeer Gripweed was not a large one, John was certainly the main draw for many, although the antiwar film must have proved a bit of a shock to those expecting to see something

OPPOSITE: The Austrian Alps made a picturesque backdrop for the "Ticket to Ride" sequence in *Help!* ABOVE, LEFT: A disguised John as seen in Help!, looking remarkably as he would in real life four years later. ABOVE, RIGHT: Ringo wore the sacrificial ring in *Help!,* in which the director made full use of his demonstrable onscreen comedic gifts.

akin to the first two Lester pictures. Mostly, the experience proved fruitful after John composed "Strawberry Fields Forever" while on location. (Likewise, Paul began his downtime from touring by composing a film score for a Boulting Brothers picture, *The Family Way,* starring Hayley Mills.)

The next time the Beatles reconvened in front of motion picture cameras was in the fall of 1967. In the two years since *Help!*, their landscape had shifted considerably in two important ways. First, they no longer toured, having made the decision to concentrate on their recording work, resulting in the landmark *Sgt. Pepper's Lonely Hearts Club Band* album. The release placed them in an even higher artistic strata. They garnered so much praise that it seemed that there was no endeavor for which they couldn't set a higher standard. Second, Brian Epstein had died (of an accidental drug overdose in August 1967), leaving them to master their collective fate alone. Both events strongly impacted their next cinematic project, *Magical Mystery Tour.*

Instead of revisiting the past glories of a Dick Lester movie for UA, Paul conceived the idea of a televised film project that the four Beatles would produce, direct, write, and star in themselves. Had Brian been alive, it is inconceivable that he would have allowed them to act upon any half-cocked

"John said, 'Magical Mystery Tour was a big ego trip for Paul.' God. It was for their sake, to keep us together, keep us going, give us something new to do...."

—Paul

estimation of their abilities. But Paul in particular felt that the Beatles needed to maintain some sort of contact with the public beyond their records. A film to air on Boxing Day (the day after Christmas) in Britain seemed a low-risk way to keep interest strong.

Inspiration came from California writer/Merry Prankster Ken Kesey (*One Flew Over the Cuckoo's Nest*), whose exploits in a psychedelically painted bus were chronicled in Tom Wolfe's *The Electric Kool-Aid Acid Test.* Paul thought that adapting the template to an English charabanc tour (wherein passengers book fares for an unnamed destination), filled with zanies as cameras rolled, would result in *something* artistically worthwhile—and perhaps even "magical."

Unfortunately, the group's golden touch did not carry over to self-generated cinema. Their apparent contempt for such niceties as planning, booking, and organizing meant that their making of the film was as chaotic as the results, souring some within the ranks. *Magical Mystery Tour* gave critics in England the chance they had long awaited to bash the Beatles unmercifully. ("Blatant rubbish!" one reviewer opined.) Lacking much coherence (by design), it was—at best—ahead of its time, presaging *Monty Python* in some respects. But it was woefully unsuited for general audiences, being an odd

OPPOSITE, TOP: Ringo would recall that the Beatles, while filming *Help!,* spoiled many a take with their marijuana-induced haze. OPPOSITE, LEFT: Richard Lester's *How I Won the War,* starring a pre-*Phantom of the Opera* Michael Crawford, was referenced by John in *Sgt. Pepper's* "A Day in the Life." ABOVE: As Paul himself would later assert, seeing the Beatles perform John's "I Am the Walrus" made *Magical Mystery Tour* not entirely worthless.

ABOVE: George was one of five (with the addition of roadie Mal Evans) wizards seen in *Magical Mystery Tour.* OPPOSITE: Geared toward kids while working on many levels, *Yellow Submarine* naturally generated many spin-off products, including this comic book and toy submarine.

blend of psychedelia and old-time British music hall entertainment. The music, though, was top-notch. Paul's "The Fool on the Hill" and George's "Blue Jay Way" made for evocative video sequences. John's song "I Am the Walrus" stands among his finest work, being a simultaneously send-up and embodiment of Summer of Love psychedelia.

No less trippy was the next theatrical release featuring the Beatles' name, though their actual involvement was limited to supplying the music. Al Brodax was a successful purveyor of Saturday morning cartoons (though in this case success refers to "monetary" rather than "artistic"). In 1964, he secured the rights to the Beatles' songs and images to produce a series that codified their *A Hard Day's Night* personas, with the dunce quotient seriously upped for Ringo. Though Brian Epstein was so appalled at the bargain-basement quality of the animation and content that he refused to allow it to be screened in the UK, he was amenable to a deal for a full-size animated feature film to be produced by Brodax.

Yellow Submarine, released in 1968, was co-scripted by Erich Segal (soon to be famous for penning *Love Story*). Bereft of any actual input from the

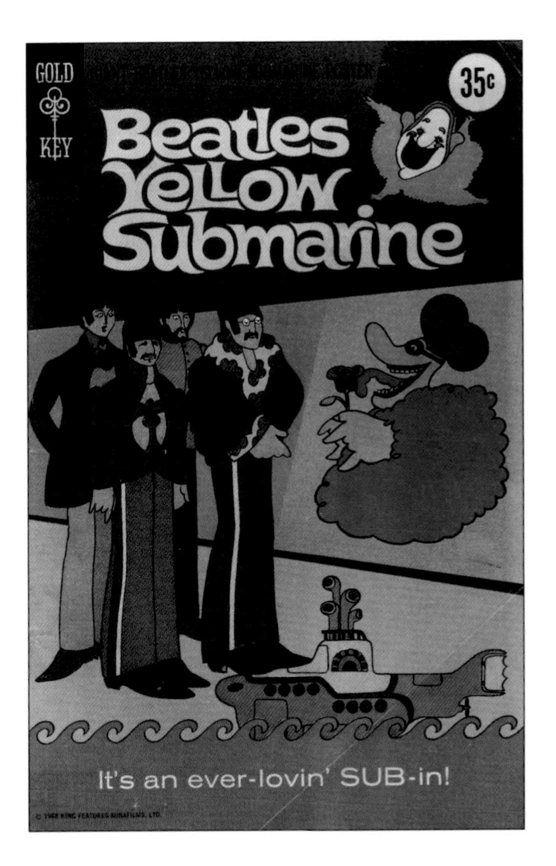

group, the filmmakers nonetheless managed to cobble together a classic "good versus evil" fantasy drawn from songs old and new that offered up the semblance of an actual story—something lacking in *Magical Mystery Tour.* Though the Beatles did not even provide their own voices for their cartoon counterparts, they did offer up some new songs (albeit "orphaned" material that they felt didn't warrant release on an actual album) and appeared as themselves for a short bit at the end.

The Beatles had hoped that their minute-long cameo would give allow them to claim *Yellow Submarine* as their contract-fulfilling third United Artists film, but that hope was quickly dashed by the studio. As 1969 dawned, it was evident that the long-anticipated end to the Beatles' run was coming into sight, as relationships were fraying within the once-tight unit. Sensing this, Paul, who had by now become the group's resident cheerleader, floated the

Fab Fact

George was voiced in *Yellow Submarine* by one "Peter Batten." Weeks before his work was completed, the "actor" was taken into custody—he had been, in fact, a deserter from the British Army who, miraculously, passed the audition. Paul Angelis, who voiced Paul and the chief Blue Meanie, completed the part.

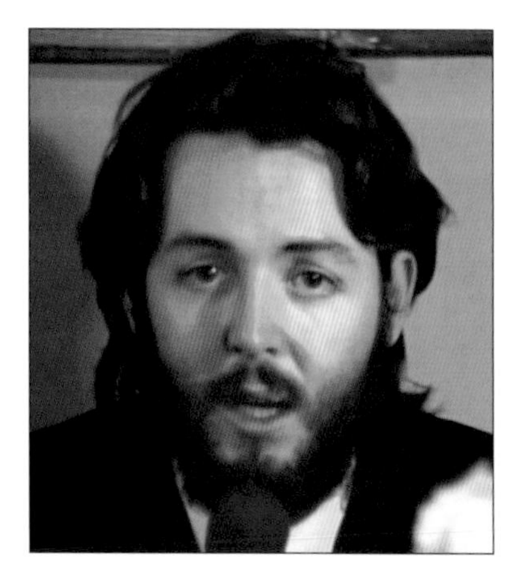

idea that a return to the band's club roots might be just the thing to sweep aside years of accumulated baggage.

By staging an unannounced appearance in an intimate venue, the Beatles could once again work their magic on an audience up-close while wowing the world with their daring. Plus, the whole thing—rehearsals and all—would be documented on celluloid for eventual broadcast as a behind-the-scenes special on television. There would be no scripts, no actors—just the Beatles themselves, being themselves.

Thus, it was with the best of intentions that the Beatles embarked on their final collective film—and what would become a serious open wound at the start of their final year of operation. Originally referred to as the "Get Back" project (after a song of Paul's that literally came into creation before the cameras), the documentary would be retitled *Let It Be* by the time the loose ends were tied up. As conceived, the film would capture the Beatles at work, rehearsing new material in preparation for a live performance that would serve as a fitting climax. But coming so quickly after their double *White Album* had been completed, the group's energies flagged, and the inhospitable environment in which they were compelled to set up at an early hour (to accommodate a film crew) at Twickenham Film Studios brought simmering tensions to the surface.

As depicted in the final cut, the few moments of documented playfulness were overshadowed by moments of peevishness, leavened by lethargy. This was not the exuberant foursome who had taken the world by storm just five years before, but individuals bored with themselves and each other. (In a striking contrast to his normal onscreen presence, Ringo is shown throughout as especially suffering from ennui.)

The club date idea long abandoned, the Beatles could not agree on a suitable venue at which to end the project. Ultimately, they settled on the rooftop of their Apple office building on Savile Row. There, during a cold January lunch hour, they worked their magic before the public one last time. Though heard, they could not be seen except by those on adjacent roofs. As a fitting finale, it worked onscreen. As the conclusion to their film career, the moment was bittersweet.

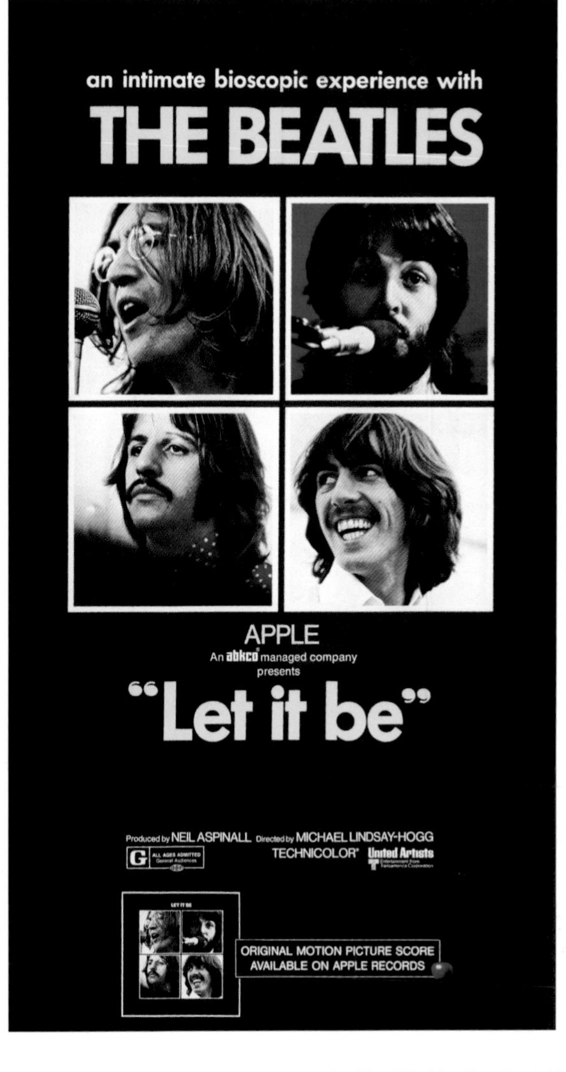

OPPOSITE, TOP: The Beatles (with Yoko) work on the film *Let It Be* on the tense soundstage of Twickenham Film Studios. OPPOSITE, BOTTOM: Like *Magical Mystery Tour, Let It Be* was Paul's baby, stirring resentment from John. ABOVE: *Let It Be*'s director, Michael Lindsay-Hogg, went back some years with the Beatles, having worked on the British rock showcase *Ready Steady Go!*

The film, which was reformatted for theatrical release (thereby meeting their outstanding obligation), opened just after the group's disintegration. The irony was that this effort to strengthen the band had exactly the opposite effect, exacerbating ill will while capturing the disunity for all the world to see. This fact was not lost on any of the participants, all of whom were no-shows at the premiere.

THE BEATLES WOMEN

"I did feel embarrassed. Walking about, married. It was like walking about with odd socks on, or your fly open."
—John

From mid-1964 to mid-1968—what most would regard as the Beatles' golden era—there was constancy in the women closest to them. While two members were betrothed to local girls, the group's burgeoning stardom granted passage into a higher social echelon for the other two. Ultimately none of the pairings lasted, but for those years the women beside these young men became nearly as famous as the Beatles themselves.

The former Cynthia Powell met John in art college, wherein the talented but unassuming "posh" girl from the right side of the tracks was widely believed to be out of the league of the brash bohemian John Lennon. But theirs was an attraction of opposites, and "Cyn," as she was called, dyed her hair blonde to maintain John's interest. (He was, as were his bandmates, particularly fixated on Brigitte Bardot as the female ideal.)

Cyn became completely devoted to her complex boyfriend. They had their shortsightedness in common, as well as the premature loss of a parent to bond them. But ultimately, both conceded that they likely would have drifted apart over time, had Cynthia's unexpected pregnancy not arisen in summer 1962. Without a second thought, John "proposed": "We'll have to get married." (John's Aunt Mimi, who had never warmed to her nephew's girlfriend, was livid with his decision to do the right thing, absenting herself and all his relatives from the ceremony.)

George and Pattie Harrison flash their smiles just after their January 21, 1966, wedding. Before popping the question, George had to make sure that the Beatles' schedule was clear. Pattie recalled George's proposal thusly: "Brian says it's okay. Will you marry me?"

The nuptials took place during a civil ceremony on August 23, one day after the Beatles were filmed at the Cavern with newly installed drummer Ringo Starr. Brian Epstein served as best man, paid for the meal, and placed the couple in an apartment at his expense. In return, news of the marriage

"John didn't get a real chance to be first a real husband or later, a real father. Once he got on the Beatles bandwagon, he couldn't get off, even if he wanted to."

—Cynthia Lennon

ABOVE: Cynthia Lennon was forced to endure a life in the shadows, at least initially, by manager Brian Epstein (*rear*). Once son Julian arrived, she became his primary caregiver, with John away on tour or working constantly. OPPOSITE: Ringo's teenaged bride, the former Maureen Cox, successfully juggled the dual roles of raising their three children while availing herself to her husband's unpredictable schedule.

(and by extension, John's pending fatherhood) was kept under wraps. Brian felt that any suggestion that any Beatle was "off-limits" would dent their popularity among the fan base.

Ringo met his first wife shortly after becoming a Beatle. Maureen (born Mary) Cox had just turned 16 when she caught a glimpse of her future husband at the Cavern. On a dare, she kissed him—but only after kissing Paul first. In fact, it was the drummer who got the young hairdresser's heart a-beating, and the two began quietly dating. They stayed steady during his remaining time in Liverpool, but as the Beatles' career took off, the enforced separation cooled the relationship. Not until 1964 and Ringo's tonsillitis did they reconnect; this time, a more lasting commitment was made.

Ringo and Paul rivaled each other as the biggest fan favorites, and it was for her own personal safety that a lid was kept on Maureen's involvement with Ringo. In fact, on more than one occasion she was accosted and viciously attacked by girls envious of her position. But with the Beatles' ascension to superstardom, opportunities for assault lessened. Ringo and Maureen married in February 1965.

Though she and the other Beatles' significant others bonded and began enjoying each other's company while their men went off to conquer the world, Maureen played the role of "Northern" wife to perfection, maintaining the household and making sure that Ringo always had a hot meal to come home to, no matter what the hour. Zak, their first child, was born in September 1965. (Zak would grow up to become one of rock's most dynamic and inspired powerhouse drummers. This despite his father's wish that he *not* follow in his footsteps.) Jason came along in 1967, followed by daughter Lee in 1970.

Though the Starkey marriage survived the tumultuous Beatlemania years, the group's traumatic breakup took a toll on its members and, by extension, the couple's relationship. An infamous 1970s incident in which George

Fab Fact

Perhaps the rarest Frank Sinatra record in existence, limited to a single pressing and designated Apple 1, was a one-off tribute done exclusively for Maureen Starkey in 1968. Knowing what a Sinatra fan his wife was, Ringo called in some favors that resulted in Old Blue Eyes recording "The Lady Is a Champ"—with customized lyrics—as a birthday present.

"Some followed me out and started kicking me again. I told them to stop. 'Who do you think you are?' they asked. They were such horrid little girls."

—Pattie Boyd, on being attacked by a group of teenage fans in 1965

ABOVE: Though Pattie Boyd (*right*) only had eyes for George, John (seen leering here in *A Hard Day's Night*) had eyes for Pattie. At a 1967 party, his less than discreet attention to George's wife brought a public slap-down from the singer Lulu. OPPOSITE, LEFT: Sophisticated and worldly, Jane Asher brought Paul up to speed in all matters of art and culture. OPPOSITE, RIGHT: The same year that the Beatles debuted in *A Hard Day's Night,* Jane appeared opposite Vincent Price in Roger Corman's *The Masque of the Red Death.* In 1966, she starred in *Alfie,* a star-making role for Michael Caine.

declared that he was in love with "Mo" chilled things in an already troubled pairing, and they divorced in 1975. Despite their ups and downs, Ringo was at her bedside when Maureen died in 1994 from complications of leukemia.

Of the four, Paul was undoubtedly *the* most popular with the ladies (or as John observed, "we knew the score"). He would hold onto his bachelorhood the longest, but for a time he was expected to enter into a power marriage with established stage and screen actress Jane Asher. Jane had been a pro since childhood, transitioning smoothly into ingénue roles by the time she met Paul in 1963. For the comparatively unsophisticated but upward striving Liverpudlian, Jane was the embodiment of cultured worldliness: Her father was a renowned doctor, and her mother was a classically trained musician. Peter Asher, her older brother, was a singer, forming one half of the pop duo Peter & Gordon.

Through Jane, Paul was given a crash course in art and theater. After missing a train back to Liverpool in early 1964, the Beatle was invited by

Mrs. Asher to make their guest room his London home. This he did, until buying a home of his own near EMI's Abbey Road Studios in 1966, where the couple thereupon set up a household. But despite their closeness (and the inspiration Jane provided for numerous songs, beginning with "And I Love Her"), there were issues between them.

To begin with, being in a relationship just short of marriage didn't preclude seeking transient female company, at least according to Paul. (Truth be told, his fellow Beatles—married or not—were equally flexible in their fidelities.) With Jane frequently away on theatrical tours, Paul never lacked companionship, though he was at least discreet about it. More problematic was his view that a wife didn't need to have an outside career—she should be devoted to taking care of the husband, house, and kids. This Jane was not buying, and though eventually the couple's engagement was publicly announced at Christmas 1967, she reached her limit months later when

Fab Fact

Well before she came into the Beatles' orbit, Jane Asher scored a hit record herself. She appeared in the title role on a spoken-word recording of *Alice in Wonderland*, issued in 1958 in England on Decca—the same label that would turn the group down four years later.

she returned to their home unexpectedly to find Paul in bed with another woman.

George met his bride while in the line of Beatle duty, on the first day's shooting of *A Hard Day's Night.* Patricia Anne Boyd was a model, known to English TV viewers as the toothy girl in the Smith's Crisps adverts. Her agent sent her to an audition in early 1964, where she found Dick Lester, who had directed the Smith's ad. She assumed that this was a similar project, but when told that it was for a small role in the Beatles' first film, she was mortified to learn that she would be wearing a schoolgirl's uniform for the part.

Since the movie was shot more or less in sequence, the two found themselves before the cameras during the train scene. Pattie's single line ("Prisoners!") was hardly memorable in and of itself, but the blonde beauty certainly caught George's eye. Despite her engagement (to a fellow named Eric), she eventually succumbed to George's persistence and had dinner with him. (Though not exactly a Beatles fan—yet—Pattie recalled later that he was the most gorgeous man she'd ever met.)

The pair hit it off and Pattie joined the inner circle, going on holiday with the others while trying to keep the relationship secret. Like Maureen, she too faced bodily harm from fans. But unlike Mrs. Starkey, she had a hard time giving up her career after the couple wed in January 1966. George, Northern to the core, didn't want her to continue modeling, so Pattie gamely tried to occupy herself in other pursuits.

One was transcendental meditation, not yet a widely known phenomenon. After sharing her interest with George, something inside him awoke. Study of the methods espoused by Maharishi Mahesh Yogi dovetailed with the interest he already had developed with the sitar—and by extension, Eastern culture in general. Thus it was that by turning on her husband, Pattie turned on the Beatles and, thereafter, Western youth culture. Over time, however, George's interest in the Krishna religion took on the characteristics of zealotry while hers remained more casual. Along with other issues, it eventually divided the couple, leading her to take up with rock star Eric Clapton, George's best friend.

ABOVE: Bob Crewe scored an instrumental smash with "Music to Watch Girls By" in 1967. His follow-up, with a British twist, was titled (naturally) *Music to Watch Birds By* and featured Pattie on the cover. OPPOSITE, LEFT: Well before she met John, Yoko Ono published a book of "instructional poems" called *Grapefruit.* Its quirky appeal likely meshed quite well with readers of John's books. OPPOSITE, RIGHT: Photographer Linda Eastman's ability to document rock stars won her an invite to Brian Epstein's home for the *Sgt. Pepper* album's launch party, days after she first met Paul.

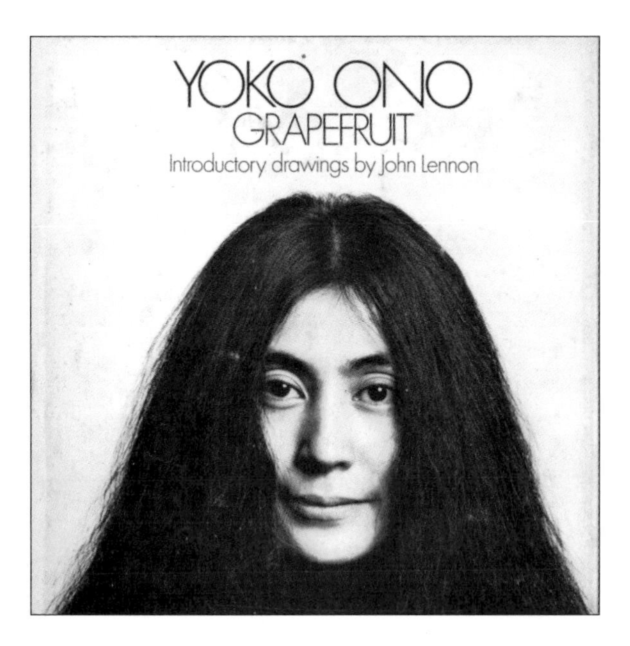

As the group's career trajectory began to wobble in the wake of Brian Epstein's death in 1967, the personal lives of the two Beatles most responsible for their success became increasingly unsettled. John had long found domestic life within his home in the stockbroker belt stifling, and he began looking outward for some stimulation. A chance encounter with a Japanese conceptual artist at London's Indica Gallery in November 1966 initiated a correspondence that would culminate in what has been spun as one of the 20th century's great love stories.

Yoko Ono was well known within art circles as a provocative and sometimes witty stager of "happenings." Based in New York, her notoriety among the Andy Warhol crowd preceded her involvement with the most outspoken Beatle. Within six months time, Paul met another New Yorker, rock photographer Linda Eastman, at London's Bag O'Nails club. The two had a brief liaison before going their separate ways, but Paul would not soon forget the woman's easygoing ways, coupled with sophistication about the ways of the business. (Her father and brother were both entertainment lawyers.)

The impact both women had on their respective men, and thereafter the Beatles, would prove pivotal in the years just ahead.

1966–1970

THE PINNACLE AND BEYOND

CONTROVERSY AND PSYCHEDELIA

Question: "In a recent article, Time *magazine...referred to 'Day Tripper' as being about a prostitute...and 'Norwegian Wood' as being about a lesbian. I just wanted to know what your intent was when you wrote it, and what your feeling is about the* Time *magazine criticism of the music that is being written today?"*

Paul: "We were just trying to write songs about prostitutes and lesbians, that's all."

In March 1966, the *London Evening Standard* ran a profile of John Lennon entitled "How Does a Beatle Live?" The article was just that, a dispassionate description of a day in the life of John as he went about his non-Beatle business. The emerging portrait detailed someone who was equal parts smug and bored while enumerating his *many* possessions. Throughout, John offered random misanthropic observations: "I couldn't stand ugly people even when I was five. Lots of the ugly ones are foreign, aren't they?"

The reporter, Maureen Cleave, was a close friend of the group (and rumored to be *very* close to John in particular), but the article was hardly flattering. In England, it came and went without much notice. In America, however, some offhand observations were reprinted in a youth magazine called *Datebook* a few months later, touching off a firestorm in America's Bible Belt over what appeared to be blasphemous arrogance. That his remarks were deliberately stripped of context mattered not, as they gave detractors an issue that they could at last use to cut the Beatles down to size.

While characterizing John as given to capricious opinions, Cleave quoted his aside on Christianity thusly: "It will vanish and shrink. I needn't argue

On the night of the Beatles' final concert, this group of protesters picketed outside Candlestick Park in San Francisco. Though it is doubtful that John Lennon or the others saw them, their presence certainly had no impact on the group's decision to make that show their last.

NOT
BEATLES TODAY, WHAT TOMORROW?
LOOK UP NOT DOWN
no other
GODS
before
SAVE the
JESUS LOVES YOU DO THE BEATLES ?
$100,000 FREE PRIZES!
THE ROYAL'S
WORLD
SEASON PARKING
CHARTER BUSES
GENERAL PARKING

Fab Fact

One day after Texas radio station KLUE organized a Beatle burning to protest John's "blasphemy," a lightning bolt struck the station's transmission tower, knocking the news director unconscious and destroying their broadcast equipment.

about that; I'm right and I will be proved right. We're more popular than Jesus now; I don't know which will go first—rock 'n' roll or Christianity. Jesus was all right but his disciples were thick and ordinary. It's them twisting it that ruins it for me." It wasn't his negative take on The Twelve or prediction that the religion wouldn't last that offended; it was his assertion that the church of Beatles held more sway among the young than Jesus did.

It didn't take long for the story to go viral, as radio stations largely confined to the American South spun his remarks as the supercilious gloating

of a spoiled, long-haired rock star crowing about his celebrity as measured against the Lord. (Ironically, the implicit suggestion that American teens would be influenced by John's words to turn away from the church only tended to reinforce his point.) The timing for the controversy couldn't have been worse, breaking just days before the Beatles were due to kick off their third stateside tour. For the first time, the group was facing serious hostility from a segment of the American population.

Brian Epstein attempted to stamp out the wildfires erupting across the country. (There were *literally* bonfires being staged in various cities, though George noted the foolishness of such movements by observing that people had to first *buy* the product in order to burn it, rendering the supposed boycott somewhat ill-conceived.) Epstein, sick with a flu, nonetheless traveled to the States to address the media and point out that what John was being accused of wasn't exactly what he had said. But Epstein's attempts to reason with those determined to be outraged did not satisfy.

Instead, in Chicago on August 11, John—alongside his bandmates—faced the media, who were eager to hear his side (while not wasting any oppor-

OPPOSITE: Birmingham, Alabaman, deejay Tommy Charles lays waste to a copy of *A Hard Day's Night* (well, the sleeve anyway) while Doug Layton similarly manhandles *Something New,* all in the name of letting John Lennon know what for after his comments on Christianity. ABOVE, LEFT: Fort Oglethorpe, Georgia, was the site of this Beatles bonfire, one day after most offended parties had accepted John's apology. ABOVE, RIGHT: John's remarks were distributed in America in *Datebook* magazine, which also ran a comment on its cover from Paul on American racism that seemingly escaped everyone's attention.

"You can't keep quiet about anything that's going on in the world, unless you're a monk." [Brief pause.] "Sorry, monks! I didn't mean it! I meant actually..."

—John, in the wake of the "Bigger than Jesus" controversy

tunity to take him down a peg or two). Though taking pains to contrast attitudes toward religion in England versus America, John sensed that his nuance was falling on deaf ears. ("Would you say you're being crucified?" a reporter asked.) Through gritted teeth, the besieged Beatle issued what no one would let him escape without: an apology. "I'm sorry I said it, really," he offered. However, he ruefully noted, "If I'd said television was bigger than Jesus, I might've gotten away with it."

The controversy came off the heels of other news stories that year that similarly placed the Beatles in a bad light. Months before, the foursome willingly posed for photographer Bob Whittaker for a rather *outré* series of images. Departing from the rather standard playful or pretty shots that made up most of their pictorial representation, Whitaker's latest concept was somewhat wooly, but visually arresting. Most attention centered on the frames that saw the group posed in butcher's smocks, with slabs of meat and dismembered baby doll parts arranged around them.

In response to a request from Capitol for a new sleeve image, the Beatles offered up one of the Whitaker pictures. Without a second thought, the

ABOVE: Though giving flippant remarks in service of the memorable quote was his stock-in-trade, seeing his remarks manipulated by people who should have known better steeled John's determination to end the spectacle that the Beatles' tours had become. OPPOSITE, TOP: The so-called "Butcher Cover" was an iconic image just ahead of its time. OPPOSITE, BELOW: The hysteric fear of Communist subversion of America had pretty much died out by 1966—until "a leftist" named Lennon opened his mouth.

photo was rushed off to the pressing plant for a U.S.-only release entitled *Yesterday and Today.* The album was a compilation of tracks siphoned off the British *Help!* and *Rubber Soul* releases (as well as both sides of the "Day Tripper"/"We Can Work It Out" single). The infamous "Butcher Cover" was taken by many as the group's commentary on how their work was sliced and diced in the States. The near apoplectic reaction from radio stations and retailers over the shockingly gruesome photo prompted Capitol to issue a recall. The company slapped an innocuous replacement shot over the offending image and issued apologies all around. *Time* called the event "a serious lapse in taste," while John spoke for the group when he declared the cover "as relevant as Vietnam."

Then there was the incident in Manila on July 4, 1966. On the final leg of their jaunt across Europe and thereon to the Pacific, the Beatles played the biggest show of their career at an outdoor venue before 80,000 Filipinos. Unbeknownst to them, however, an invite to appear at the presidential palace went un-RSVPed. Nonetheless, First Lady Imelda Marcos, wife of strong-arm leader Ferdinand Marcos, carried on as if they *had* agreed to show for the luncheon, allowing TV camera crews and a crowd of three hundred children to show up at the royal palace.

When the Beatles failed to appear, due to one snafu or another in the chain of protocol, the incident was reported as "Beatles snub Imelda." With the nation's honor stained thusly, all goodwill evaporated immediately. All amenities were withdrawn, along with the band's take of the shows. En route to the airport and a quick getaway, the Beatles and their entourage were subjected to jostling, jeers, and physical blows from angry mobs and service workers, followed by the forced grounding of their plane before takeoff. The group later described the ordeal as terrifying.

Back in England, George was asked at a news conference what the future held. "We're going to have a couple of weeks to recuperate before we go and get beaten up by the Americans," he said. His flip answer was more prescient than he knew at the time, but it was indicative of the entire band's weariness with touring. Each member was acutely aware of his deteriorating musicianship when compelled to perform before throngs that would

Fab Fact

The title for *Revolver* came only after much debate within the group, as no one agreed on any other suggestion. Early contenders included *Abracadabra, The Beatles on Safari,* and Ringo's facetious offering: *Aftergeography,* a play on the Rolling Stones' recent *Aftermath.*

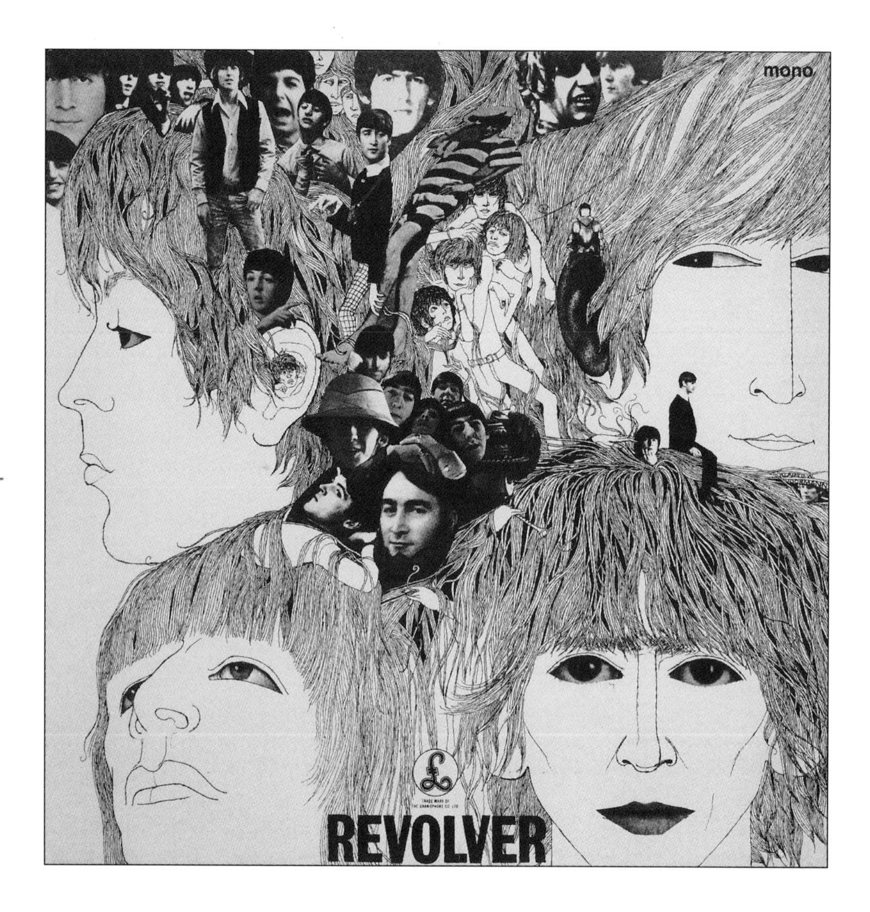

not allow them to hear themselves. Outside conditions that placed them at the mercy of demanding promoters and outlandish attempts at security (the Beatles found themselves trapped inside an armored car that summer when the exit from a venue was unexpectedly locked) had at last pushed them past their limits.

At the same time, their artistry was growing by leaps and bounds. *Rubber Soul,* issued at the end of 1965, was widely seen as their first truly mature work. While Paul's "Michelle" extended his streak of increasingly sophisticated pop standards, John's "Girl" likewise detailed a complexity of emotions unforecast by the fare they had routinely cranked out just two years earlier. Another track, "The Word," portended the universal love theme that would see full expression with "All You Need Is Love" a mere eighteen months later. What most of the diverse offerings had in common was little chance of translating to the concert stage.

On 1966's *Revolver,* nearly all of the arrangements transcended the capabilities of a standard four-man lineup to pull them off outside the studio. Recordings replete with strings, horn sections, tape loops, and even Indian instrumentation populated the release, which was issued days before the group landed on U.S. soil. Then as now, it was unthinkable for an act to go out on the road without supporting its newest product. But the Beatles didn't need to sell records to survive; their final tour in 1966 was really more about fulfilling the demand for personal appearances than to showcase their latest work. Before the American jaunt was over, they had already answered the question they had asked themselves while engaged thusly: What was the point of touring?

As far as any Beatle could see, there wasn't one. Their comfort level with George Martin and the recording studio's capabilities was cresting. *Revolver* represented an even further advance over its predecessor, as the group now

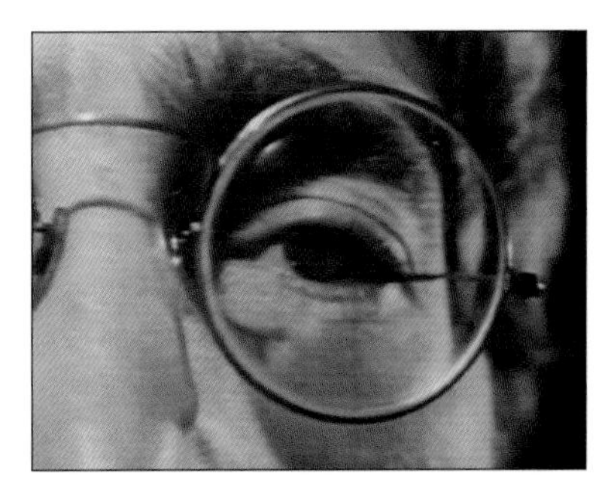

OPPOSITE: *Revolver,* featuring a cover designed by the Beatles' old Hamburg friend, Klaus Voormann, was seriously hobbled in America by the removal of three Lennon songs, which had been siphoned off months earlier to round out *Yesterday and Today.* LEFT and ABOVE: The images of George and John seen here, as well as of Ringo and Paul on the following pages, are from the groundbreaking music video for "Strawberry Fields Forever," directed by Swedish filmmaker Peter Goldman (who had been recommended by Klaus).

ABOVE: George's infatuation with all things Indian took several forms, including spiritual, cultural, and musical. His commitment to playing the sitar culminated with lessons from the world's greatest player, Ravi Shankar (*pictured*). OPPOSITE, LEFT: The "Paperback Writer"/"Rain" single marked a technological advance in the Beatles' sound. Paul's muscular bass line was brought more forward in the mix, while on the flip the group experimented with backwards tapes for the first time.

openly experimented with not just composition but with the sonic settings of their work. "Backwards tape" effects—literally turning the tape back to front, resulting in sounds otherwise incapable of being achieved—was now a standard tool in their arsenal, as was vari-speed: speeding up or slowing down the recording playback, per the needs of the song and the desired effect.

While Martin was, to his credit, as avid an enabler as they could have wished for—taking their fancies and making them tangible—some of their artistic breakthrough can be traced to the group's experimentation with psychedelics. A mutual friend had dosed John and George with LSD in 1965.

Though their first trip came against their will, they were quick to acknowledge what they felt were the unmistakable benefits, at least when it came to broadening their perceptions. Said George: "The only way I could begin to describe it is like an astronaut on the moon, or in his space ship, looking back at the Earth. I was looking back to the Earth from my [heightened] awareness."

Though they never made it a practice to overtly advocate drug use (beyond adding their name to petitions calling for decriminalization), the Beatles were not shy about offering up songs that certainly evoked the Technicolor experiences they had enjoyed while under the influence. Perhaps the earliest was John's "Rain," issued as the flip to Paul's "Paperback Writer" in the spring of 1966. Through the use of backwards tape and a slowed-down backing track, John turned the banality of precipitation into a metaphor

"We have a special man who sits here and goes like this. [He indicates twisting knobs at a recording console.] And the guitar turns into a piano or something. And then you may say, 'Why don't you use a piano?' Because the piano sounds like a guitar."

—Ringo, on record production

Fab Fact

Attendance for the Beatles' last American tour was down from the year before, with many venues only two-thirds filled. The Candlestick Park show lost money for the promoters, as only 25,000 of more than 42,000 available tickets were sold, at a top price of $6.50.

that suggested that one's reaction to external forces was "just a state of mind."

On *Revolver,* he actually recounted an acid trip. "She Said She Said" told how actor Peter Fonda's insistence on describing his own death on the operating table so unnerved John that he was made to feel "like I've never been born." But the album's most hallucinatory track was based on John's reading of *The Egyptian Book of the Dead.* "Tomorrow Never Knows" (titled after another Ringo malapropism) came all tricked out with a trance-inducing drum pattern, sonic effects (courtesy of tape loops) that came and went randomly, and a detached Lennon vocal achieved in part by running his voice through a rotating Leslie organ speaker. That a mainstream pop act would place so avant-garde a recording on an album indicates that the Beatles were confident that their fans would follow wherever they led.

Other tracks were equally groundbreaking. George's "Love You To," which marked his first excursion into raga rock, was entirely supported by Indian instruments—previously unheard of in rock music. Though he was regarded as the junior partner within the group, George's steady growth as a writer came to full bloom with this release, as three of his songs made the cut. One, "Taxman," became the Beatles' first explicit political commentary on record. Paul offered up his strongest set of material yet, including the Dickensian tale of loneliness, "Eleanor Rigby"; a Beach Boys pastiche, "Here, There and Everywhere"; and an homage to pot, doubling as a joyous, Motown-esque love song: "Got to Get You into My Life." Even Ringo was given a worthy star turn with "Yellow Submarine," a sing-along tune designed for kids, but with fittingly reflective lyrics (contributed in part by British pop star Donovan).

That the Beatles could go out on tour and utterly ignore *Revolver*'s existence seemed a subtle way of telegraphing their intent to retire from performing that year. It should be noted that precedent for a pop act to subsist entirely on its recorded output didn't really exist. For the Beatles to take this great leap into the unknown showed remarkable confidence in their abilities to create something in the studio that would eclipse the demand for live appearances. Events bore them out.

The end came on August 29, 1966, at San Francisco's Candlestick Park. Paul tipped off press agent Tony Barrow that the show would be their last and that he might want to tape it with his portable recorder. (Barrow did, but the tape ran out before the set did.) Just after they closed with "Long Tall Sally," an unscripted nod to their Cavern days, John picked the opening notes to "In My Life" before departing the stage as a Beatle for the last time. The Beatles returned to England, went their separate ways for the first time in years over the next couple of months, and then reconvened at their EMI stomping grounds in December.

The first product of their liberation from the road came in the form of a remarkable single comprised of John and Paul's look back at their respective childhoods. Paul's "Penny Lane" was, predictably, sunny and catchy, but deceptively complex. The song's signature flavor came from a "piccolo trumpet"—a rarely heard instrument that had caught Paul's attention during a TV broadcast of Beethoven's Brandenburg Concerto. Balancing the song (the release was officially designated as a "double A-side") was John's "Strawberry Fields Forever," a surreal, impressionistic composition that gathered images originating in childhood as the starting to point to an exploration of the inner psyche. It too utilized an uncommon instrument: the Mellotron, a precursor to electronic synthesizers.

OPPOSITE: The Beatles played before many empty seats during their final year on tour, even at the 1966 Shea Stadium concert seen here. ABOVE, TOP: The end came on an uncharacteristically cold evening in San Francisco. ABOVE: Paul grew a mustache in early 1966 to cover a scar on his upper lip, incurred during a moped accident.

ABOVE: Loathed by critics and loved by kids, the fabricated Monkees represented a merchandising juggernaut—just like the mop-top Beatles of the early to mid-'60s. OPPOSITE: Photographed by Michael Cooper, the *Sgt. Pepper* album cover was a lavish undertaking, featuring a design by husband-and-wife team Peter Blake and Jann Haworth, based on a concept by Robert Fraser. This outtake from the shoot was briefly available as a poster.

The tunes were pop like no one else had ever heard—or produced—before. George Martin anticipated even more fruitful achievements from this new direction but, recognizing the demands of commerce, agreed that the two tracks should be released as a stand-alone single, in advance of, rather than as a part of, the album-in-the-works—a decision he later regretted. But the Beatles weren't about to be rushed. Though the public wasn't accustomed to long waits between releases, the group's desire to get the music just so trumped any other interest.

In the interim, fans longing for the manic lightheartedness of years past could find solace in a newer phenomenon, inspired by the Beatles' film work and launched through the muscle of television. *The Monkees,* debuting in the fall of 1966, was a sitcom aimed squarely at those Beatles fans who may have felt left behind by the group's new direction. Unabashedly frothy, the show offered four actors/musicians cast as the fictitious band: Micky Dolenz, Davy Jones, Michael Nesmith, and Peter Tork.

Though recordings issued under the group name were intended purely to promote the series, they sold by the millions, as the "Pre-Fab Four" took on a life of their own. While derided by critics as the nadir of popular music, cynically contrived purely for profit, the Monkees in time developed into a true band and issued some fine records. Moreover, the Beatles themselves were fans. (In early 1967, they in fact invited the Monkees to England to visit during their ongoing recording sessions.)

The issue of sustaining themselves without touring sparked an epiphany from Paul: What if, instead of *The Beatles* going out on tour, they created a fictitious act of their own, represented purely by the collection of songs that they were working on, and *the record* went out on tour? So it was that Paul, inspired by the monikers of some West Coast bands he had seen while visiting the States, came up with *Sgt. Pepper's Lonely Hearts Club Band.*

The album issued by that name in June 1967—ten months after *Revolver*—remains perhaps the most analyzed long-player of the rock era. To merely sum up the salient points would be a lengthy exercise, but what is important to know is that its release was a cultural milestone. Just as their 1964 debut on *The Ed Sullivan Show* united millions, becoming a common "where were

"Brown paper bags for Sgt. Pepper."

—Notation by Brian Epstein, who believed the "excess" of the jacket sleeve would turn off fans

you?" moment, so too was the first hearing of *Sgt. Pepper.* Though it was commonly but inaccurately regarded as the first "concept album," *Sgt. Pepper* did boast *the suggestion* of thematic unity. Its stunning (and expensive) cover art presented what appeared to be the title act—John, Paul, George, and Ringo clad in colorful, military-type costumes—surrounded by their audience, which included "The Beatles"—their old incarnation.

The record opened with sounds associated with the start of a concert. By reprising the title tune just before the album's stunning closer, "A Day in the Life," the LP had the effect of taking listeners on a journey. Whatever else might be said, *Sgt. Pepper* was an album that invited start-to-finish listenings, rather than just selective playings of "the hits." In so doing, it changed the art of rock forever.

Fab Fact

The making of *Sgt. Pepper* required seven hundred hours of recording time over six months, with recording costs reaching £25,000. The album spent fifteen weeks at No. 1 in the U.S. and was nominated for seven Grammies, winning four.

APPLE BITES

"We really want to help people, but without doing it like a charity or seeming like ordinary patrons of the arts. We're in the happy position of not really needing any more money. So for the first time, the bosses aren't in it for profit."
—Paul, on Apple

The Beatles' Apple enterprise tapped the Dutch design collective known as The Fool often, whether for the *Sgt. Pepper* inner sleeve, the clothes marketed at their boutique, or the colorful mural that adorned the shop. This poster, *A Is for Apple,* was sold at their Baker Street store.

With the end of touring, Brian Epstein's role as a daily, hands-on manager seemed at first glance to be largely diminished, perhaps even superfluous. The Beatles' stardom was firmly established. Reporters no longer asked them "How long do you think you'll last?" anymore, as they had incessantly back in 1964. Their record deal, while hardly what it could have been, insured that no one would bother them as they ran up studio time while perfecting their latest ideas. Indeed, just as their earlier singles had transformed rock music—revitalizing it with joy and energy while pushing its boundaries—*Sgt. Pepper* almost overnight changed conceptions of what a rock album could be. Had the Beatles still been locked into the grind of tours (and making another film), it's doubtful that the album would have ever come into being in the first place.

Still, Brian believed he would continue in his role as facilitating the group's supremacy in an extremely fickle business. To that end, his final managerial act saw him get the Beatles booked as Britain's representatives for a *global* television broadcast in June 1967, *Our World.* It was the first TV broadcast viewed simultaneously around the world, utilizing the latest satellite technology. Though chosen to represent one's country would be an honor beyond comprehension for most, the Beatles had mixed feelings initially, with the fear of falling flat among them.

They needn't have worried. John Lennon rose to the occasion, penning the suitably universal "All You Need Is Love." In both melody and lyric, it was simplicity itself, encapsulating the Summer of Love gestalt beautifully.

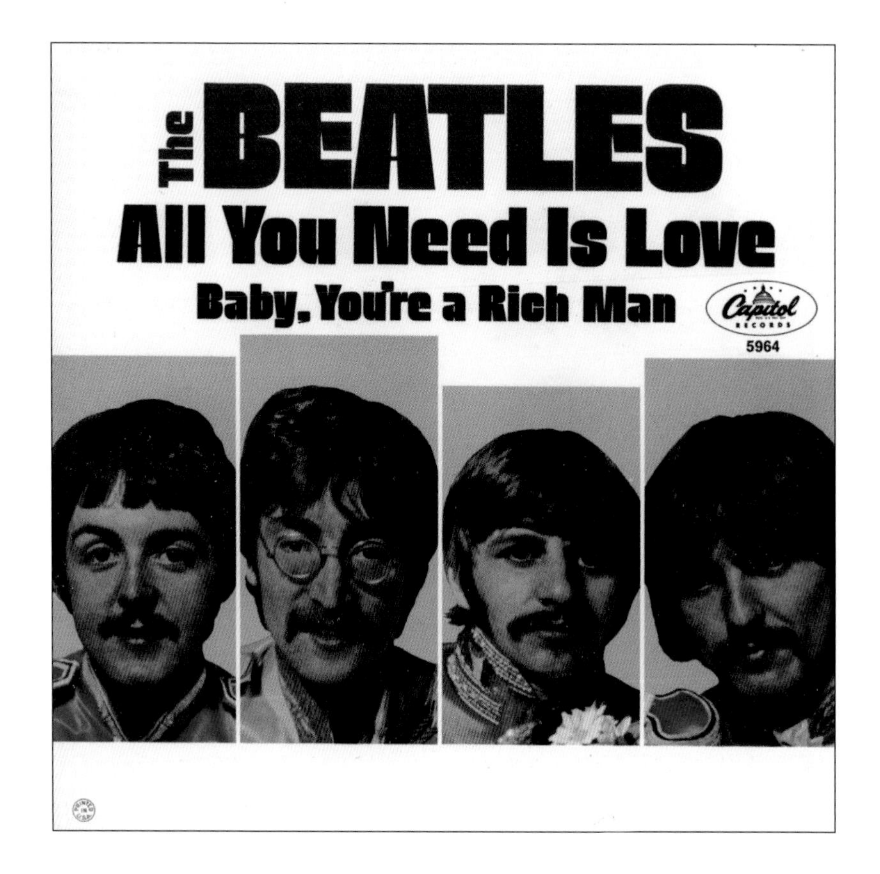

ABOVE: Though *Sgt. Pepper* spawned no hit singles upon its release, "All You Need Is Love," issued six weeks later, served as an extension of that landmark album. OPPOSITE, TOP: Apple's business office was a study in organized chaos, proving definitively that the skill set that made one a brilliant artist wasn't necessarily transferable to the boardroom. OPPOSITE, BOTTOM: The media had a field day mischaracterizing the Beatles' interest in Transcendental Meditation. *Mad* magazine offered its own satirical treatment.

More than 300 million viewers around the world watched the Beatles put finishing touches on the song at EMI's Abbey Road studio, with a supporting cast that included a full orchestra and celebrity well-wishers, among them the Rolling Stones' Mick Jagger and the Who's Keith Moon. The moment codified the meme, established by the reception to *Sgt. Pepper* only weeks before, that the Beatles were the spokesmen for a generation.

Though the event was a genuine achievement, Brian was somewhat lost in the post-touring world. He even considered selling out his business interests to Robert Stigwood, best known as the mastermind behind the success of Cream and, later, the Bee Gees. But before any decision could be made, Epstein was found dead of an accidental drug overdose. He was thirty-two. (Then as now, speculation swirled that it was a suicide, but insiders concluded that coming only weeks after his father's death, Brian would never have committed such a selfish act, as devoted to his bereaved mother as he was.)

Once past the shock of Brian's death, the consensus among the group was that they must somehow carry on. The formation of a company encompassing records, film, electronics, and clothing had been in the air for some time. With Brian's death leaving them rudderless, it was Paul who stepped up to unify them with work. Hoping to instill a sense of purpose, Paul rallied his bandmates, first with the *Magical Mystery Tour* film and then the set-up of Apple (as the enterprise would be called).

The first manifestation came with the Apple retail store on London's Baker Street. Though it is commonplace nowadays for celebrities to peddle fashion or fragrance lines, the Beatles' marketing of a clothing brand (designed by a Dutch collective called The Fool) in 1967 was a groundbreaking move. But the business quickly proved to be less than a good idea, as overpriced, instantly dated fashions were a tough sell, despite the group's cachet. Quickly tiring of being shopkeepers, the group ended things by staging a public giveaway of remaining stock on July 30, 1968.

By that time, Apple's record label was taking shape, with a roster of artists handpicked by the Beatles themselves. They included Liverpool's Jackie Lomax, an R&B singer and friend from the old days; James Taylor, an American singer/songwriter brought in by Peter Asher, by now the head of Apple artist and repertoire; and a Welsh chanteuse named Mary Hopkin, brought to Paul's attention by model/actress Twiggy.

Hopkin's star turn was launched with Paul's hands-on involvement. He selected the material and produced her himself, beginning with a haunting ballad he had found called "Those Were the Days." Under his guidance, the single became a worldwide smash in the fall of 1968, placing Apple on the map as a success, at least as far as records were concerned.

Elsewhere within the group, things were less sanguine. The year had begun with all four Beatles and their partners traveling to Rishikesh, India. The purpose of the sojourn was to immerse themselves fully in the study of Transcendental Meditation, as practiced by a fifty-year-old Indian guru, Maharishi Mahesh Yogi. Though much of the media viewed the more outlandish claims of TM's adherents with healthy skepticism, the Beatles themselves,

Fab Fact

The night before their public giveaway, the Beatles themselves showed up at their Baker Street shop, carting away as much of their merchandise as they could handle. What remained was deemed good enough for public consumption.

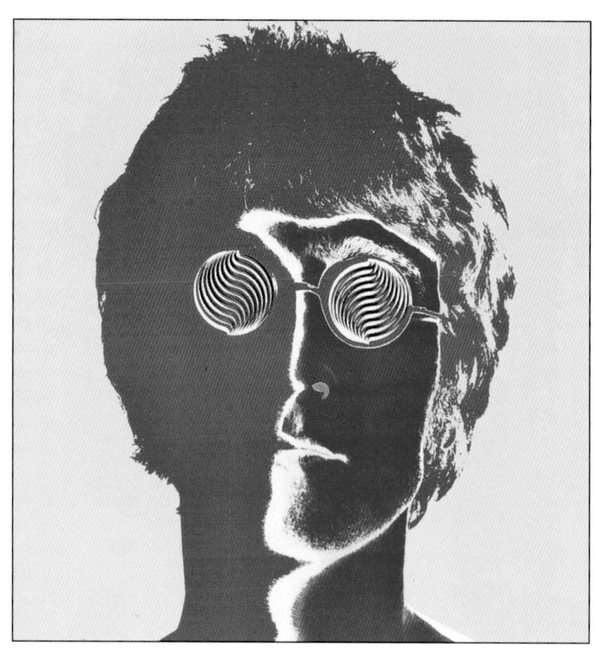

Renowned fashion photographer Richard Avedon captured these oh-so-1967 day-glo images of the four Beatles for *Look* magazine. Fans could purchase their own set by mail order.

having begun their explorations a year earlier (after exposure to the Maharishi from George's bride, Pattie) were quite sold on the idea. They credited TM as a stabilizing influence that helped bring their LSD use to an end.

But the Indian trip ended badly. First Ringo and his wife decamped after two weeks, complaining about the flies and the spicy food. (Ringo possessed a fragile digestive system, due to several childhood illnesses.) Paul and Jane Asher left not long after, though the lessons of TM stayed with him, perhaps indirectly leading to his later becoming a full-time vegetarian and nature advocate. John, not naturally given to discipline, grew restless with the hours of meditation and solitude. All it took for him to make his exit was the hint that their Holy Man was less than divine.

A provocateur within their midst, Apple electronics head "Magic" Alex Mardas, had conned his way into their inner circle and was present on the sabbatical. It was he who spread the rumor that the Maharishi had had designs on actress Mia Farrow, who along with Beach Boy Mike Love and several others was among their party. Without so much as a shred of evidence, John stormed out of the camp, followed by a dismayed George, who felt

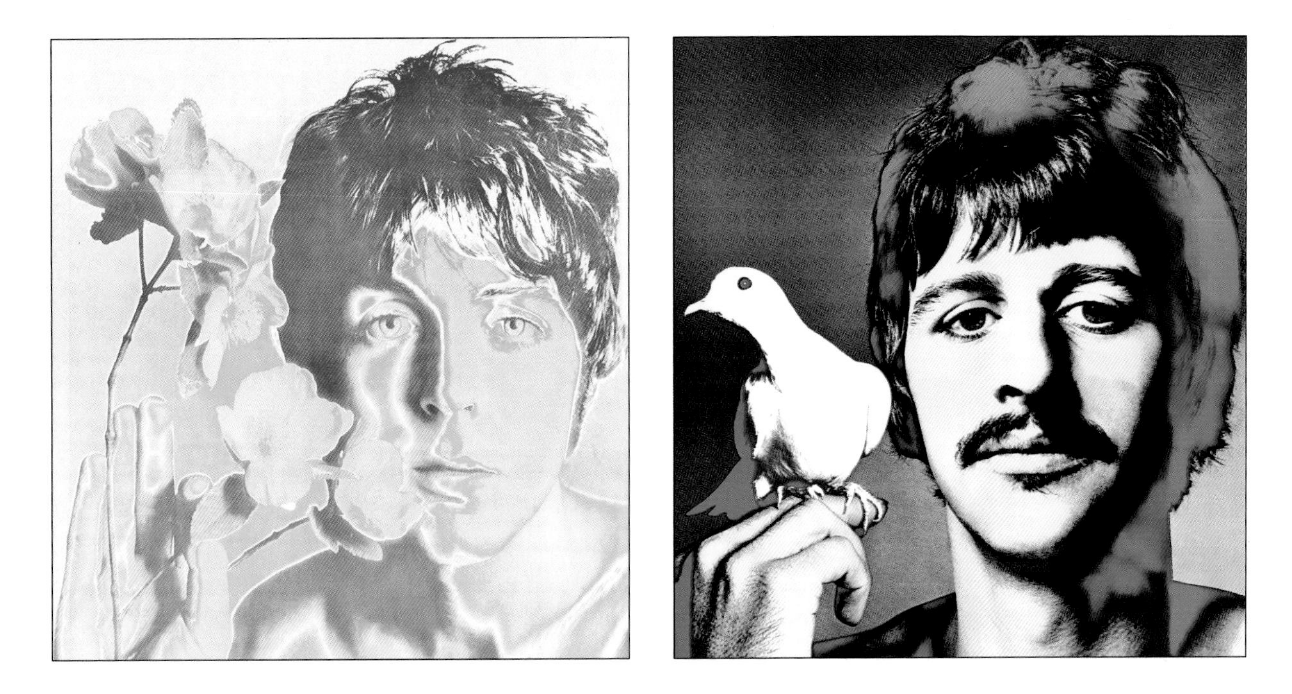

(rightly) that the guru had been unfairly maligned. Though the press had a field day mocking the Beatles for their "far out" proclivities, the experience did serve as a productive songwriting camp, away from media scrutiny and the distractions of life in London.

Between John, Paul, and George, more than thirty tunes were composed, more than enough for a double album. (Even Ringo came up with his first solely credited composition.) Eager to get their label launched with a bang (and—truth be told—operating under the delusion that a two-record set would help fulfill their contractual obligations faster), the group set about the recording of a follow-up to *Sgt. Pepper* entitled simply *The Beatles,* but known universally as the "White Album" due to its austere cover art.

Issued in advance of the set was their first single since "Lady Madonna" (released just before the India trip in February). It featured two strong compositions, one each from John and Paul. The former's topical offering was called "Revolution"; the latter's was both personal and universal. It was called "Hey Jude," and would stay at the No. 1 spot on the charts for nine weeks in late summer.

Fab Fact

Clocking in at 7:11, "Hey Jude" was the longest Beatles single, as well as the longest No. 1 record ever to that time. Bob Dylan's "Like a Rolling Stone" (6:05)—one of the first long rock songs to become a hit—had stalled at No. 2 in 1965, blocked by the Beatles' "Help!"

THE BREAKUP

"The Beatles used to be a cooperative, creative unit."
—Paul to George

"Find somebody else to be cooperative with."
—George to Paul

In May 1968, shortly after the Beatles' return from India, Cynthia Lennon went off on a brief trip to Greece. In her absence, John, just back from New York, where he and Paul had announced the formation of Apple, invited artist Yoko Ono over for the evening. She and John had been corresponding for well over a year, and thus far the secret communiqués had been of an artistically provocative nature and nothing more. On this evening, John showed Yoko his home recording facility, and through the night, the two collaborated on an avant-garde sound collage. When they finished, they capped off their "date" by consummating their relationship.

It was the subsequent breakup of the Lennons' marriage that provided Paul with the initial inspiration for "Hey Jude," which began as a song of comfort for five-year-old Julian Lennon. As the boy's "uncle," and with his natural way with children, Paul bonded with Julian in a way that John himself never could fully match, which was not altogether surprising given his own "daddy" issues. Nonetheless, when Paul played the work in progress to his songwriting partner, John took it to be about himself and his unfolding relationship with Yoko: "You have found her, now go and get her." No, Paul demurred; it's about *me.* "Check," John responded. "We're going through the same bit."

Jane Asher and Paul reached the end of their love match in July. After an interval with one Francie Schwartz, an American drawn to Apple with a film script in her pocket, Paul reached out to Linda Eastman, the single mom

The Beatles' last moment of public glory came at the least likely of places: atop their office building on Savile Row. The forty-five-minute set concluded with John's comment to the assembled: "I hope we passed the audition."

"The cartoon is this: four guys on a stage with a spotlight on them; second picture, three guys onstage, breezing out of the spotlight; third picture, one guy standing there, shouting, 'I'm leaving.'"

—John

and rock photographer with whom he had maintained sporadic contact since their meeting over a year earlier. With Yoko steering most of John's attentions away from the group, it was a most auspicious time for Paul to undertake a new romantic relationship himself.

Sessions for the *The Beatles* ("White Album") marked the most turbulent time ever for the group. Any inclination toward a common goal was rapidly

eroding, as the India experience had seemed to magnify, rather than mitigate, any ego issues. "If everyone had 'got it' in Rishikesh," opined George, "they would have been meditating more and not getting into distractions." The start-up of Apple certainly constituted a distraction from being a Beatle, but the romantic traumas surrounding the group and the sudden presence of "outsiders" into what had been the group's sanctuary quite definitely had an effect on morale.

To many, the mere mention of Yoko Ono elicits hostility, for she is frequently blamed for the group's disintegration. While the reality is far more complex, the couple's outside antics did tend to undermine any feelings of group unity. One issue that drew much attention and discomfort was John and Yoko's decision to memorialize their first date in vinyl form as *Unfinished Music No. 1: Two Virgins.* While the LP's contents posed little threat to the Beatles' public image, the nude photo of the couple on the album's jacket most certainly did. It took long months of bitter back-and-forth among the Beatles and their parent record company to finally allow the release out,

OPPOSITE: Photographer Ronald Fitzgibbon was responsible for the image gracing this issue of *Life* magazine, which contained excerpts from the Beatles' "authorized biography" by Hunter Davies. ABOVE: Seen at an Ossie Clark fashion show in August 1968, the pairing of John and Yoko was not well received by the public. The couple's non-Beatles antics, such as the infamous *Two Virgins* record sleeve, put most sympathy for the Lennon's divorce strictly in Cynthia's corner.

ABOVE, TOP: The "Hey Jude"/"Revolution" single launched Apple Records with a bang. This sleeve photo depicts the music video for the latter tune, which was directed by Michael Lindsay-Hogg. ABOVE, BOTTOM: If George Harrison felt that his fellow Beatles gave him the respect he deserved only capriciously, producer George Martin's attitude toward the youngest Beatle was worse. As Martin later admitted, "I was always rather beastly to George." OPPOSITE: Paul recognized "Hey Jude" as something special, with its extended coda inviting audience participation by singing along. The video shoot, which did just that, reawakened his desire to play before the public again.

whereupon charges of obscenity from local municipalities tended to make it one of those things more heard about than actually listened to.

With so much Beatles material to cover, work on their new album tended to be more fractious, with several recordings taking place in different studios simultaneously. In addition to taxing George Martin's abilities, the practice also led to tensions when, for instance, Paul would play all the parts himself on a track, rather than allow a group effort. George in particular suffered the indignity of being dictated to, while Ringo took any criticism to heart. He finally reached the breaking point in August, when he walked out with no intent to return. After a two-week vacation in Sardinia and much coaxing from the other three, Ringo eventually came back—to discover his drum kit covered with flowers.

Engineer Geoff Emerick *did* quit the project midway through, having his fill of the arguing and blame directed his way when things weren't going smoothly. The normally unflappable George Martin made his move in a more passive-aggressive fashion, announcing without warning that he was taking a vacation before turning over control of the sessions to twenty-one-year-old production assistant Chris Thomas.

For all the chaos that went into the making of *The Beatles,* the results were stunning. While lacking the cohesiveness of *Sgt. Pepper, The Beatles* offered the most eclectic blend of music that the group had yet committed to vinyl. From the gentle romanticism of "I Will" to the thundering wall of noise that was "Helter Skelter," Paul gave a full display of his talents as a singer and writer. George likewise acquitted himself well with four tracks, including "While My Guitar Gently Weeps," which featured the talents of Eric Clapton in a precedent-setting guest star role. Ringo's charming "Don't Pass Me By" marked his songwriting debut, while John presented an array of music ranging from the lilting "Julia," a simultaneous homage to both his mother and Yoko, to his *musique concrete,* "Revolution #9"—an at times disturbing track that challenged listeners in a way no Beatles "song" ever had.

Martin may have sensed that his authority was not what it once had been, for in the year since Brian Epstein's death, the lid that had kept egos in check and group harmony ongoing was gone. Brian's absence was felt in ways that the four might not have been fully able to articulate, but it was fast becoming clear that managing their business affairs was not a job for amateurs. Apple was fast turning into a money pit, where assets (like company cars) routinely vanished and the office on Savile Row took on the air of "the longest cocktail party" (as one employee described it), filled with freeloaders living off the Beatles' largesse.

The issue of *who* would be the Beatles' savior ironically became the wedge that would drive the four apart. After exploring a few options locally, John (with Yoko) was invited to a meeting with New Yorker Allen Klein, the Rolling Stones' business manager and a man widely known for his ability to pry unpaid royalties loose from record companies (while often feared for his hardball tactics). Klein had read of Apple's troubles and flown to London with the express purpose of taking charge of the Beatles' affairs. Though unapologetically brusque, he also was savvy enough to do his homework. He recognized that if he could win over the skeptical John, he'd stand a good shot of reaching the rest of them.

Klein didn't immediately realize that he was competing for the role alongside another New Yorker, entertainment attorney Lee Eastman, his polar opposite in temperament. Things quickly turned ugly when the normally unflappable Eastman and Klein met with the Beatles to sort things out. Klein, the street brawler, taunted Eastman unmercifully; the latter, to his detriment, took the bait, and unleashed a volley of invective that doomed any chance of cooperation between the sides. Effectively, any chance for the Beatles to work their way through their disagreements ended right there, with Lennon siding with Klein (and persuading George and Ringo as part of the bargain). Meanwhile, McCartney remained certain in his belief that Eastman (his future father-in-law) represented their best chance at getting their affairs in order.

The meeting occurred just days after the group played its final public set, on Apple's rooftop, in early 1969. No matter what business issues separated them, the rooftop concert showed that, given a challenge, the Beatles could certainly rise to the occasion when confined to purely musical matters. But their current project, a documentary film/album, left a bad taste in the

Fab Fact

Contrary to persistent rumors, Paul did not routinely replace Ringo's drum parts himself, but he did commandeer the kit on three occasions: on "Back in the U.S.S.R." and "Dear Prudence," both recorded during Ringo's walk-out, and on "The Ballad of John and Yoko," taped while George and Ringo were unavailable.

mouths of all the participants. *Let It Be,* as it would eventually be named, left in its dysfunctional wake hours and hours of film and tape that needed sorting out, and no one to take charge of it. (George Martin had limited his role to what amounted to a consultancy, given the bad time their last joint effort had been and that the *Let It Be* project wasn't intended to be a proper new album in the first place.)

The doomed effort had mutated from a "behind the scenes" view of rehearsals for a show to a "making of the album" documentary. But their original aim—to present themselves on tape raw, bereft of studio tricks and overdubbing ("as nature intended," ads for the "Get Back" single claimed)—resulted in an imperfect mess that resembled a bootleg of themselves more than an actual Beatle product. The tapes were handed over to ace producer Glyn Johns to make something salable, but few could stomach the results of his efforts.

Meanwhile, both John and Paul took a bride within days of each other in March 1969. The marriage of Paul, the last Beatles bachelor, stirred scenes

Fab Fact

As Linda Eastman was by trade a photographer, a large segment of the population concluded that she was heiress to the Eastman-Kodak fortune. In fact, her father had changed the family name to Eastman from...*Epstein.*

OPPOSITE: On March 12, 1969, Paul gave fans one last blast of Beatlemania with his wedding to Linda Eastman at the Marylebone Registry office. With stalwart employees Peter Brown (*with beard*) and Mal Evans (*behind, with glasses*) in attendance, the absence of Paul's fellow Beatles was conspicuous. ABOVE: Not to be outdone, John held his March 20 wedding to Yoko in Gibraltar and then invited the world's press to the couple's honeymoon at the Amsterdam Hilton for a week of peace chat during their "bed-in."

reminiscent of the group's Beatlemania-era heyday. His marriage to Linda Eastman in a civil ceremony at the Marylebone Register Office in London on a rainy afternoon drew hundreds of weeping fans. Not to be outdone, John and Yoko married in Gibraltar. The couple used the glare of media attention to illuminate their pet cause, world peace.

To that end, a "bed-in" was held in their honeymoon suite at the Amsterdam Hilton. For seven days, journalists were freely welcomed in to chat about anything, but mostly John and Yoko steered the conversation to the peace movement, suggesting that peace could be achieved "if you want it." As a diversion from heavier issues, this clownish story may have provoked as many as it swayed, but John didn't stop there. In June, another such event was held in Montreal, where an anthem for the movement, "Give Peace a Chance," was recorded and issued as a single, giving pacifists everywhere something substantive to use in rallies forever onward.

"There's that famous old saying: 'You always hurt the one you love.' And we all love each other and we all know that. But we still sort of hurt each other, occasionally."

—Ringo

As for the group itself, one thing was clear: With relations remaining tense among the foursome, perhaps something to cleanse the palette was in order. It fell to Paul to persuade a skeptical George Martin that the Beatles were capable of marshaling their best behavior in order to complete an album with little stress, just like "the old days." Paul was as good as his word, getting the others to agree to work together for collective rather than individual interests. In the summer of 1969, work on what became their final group effort began.

George's songwriting and confidence had grown measurably in the months since their last group session, having worked with several Apple acts as producer and sideman. *Abbey Road,* as the new album was called, contained two of his finer compositions, "Here Comes the Sun" and "Something." The latter was pulled as a single, giving the "quiet Beatle" his first A-side ever. It was issued with John's "Come Together" on the flip, a powerful return to his rock and roll roots that benefitted mightily from Paul's musical input. Ringo contributed a second solo composition, "Octopus's Garden"—a nod to "Yellow Submarine," perhaps, but an idiom that suited him well.

It was the LP's second side that drew attention as Paul's baby. About a half dozen songs, unrealized on their own, if not unfinished, were expertly stitched together to form a grand medley, or a "suite," if you will. They represented the pinnacle of Paul and George Martin's close working relationship, being a musical soundscape that took listeners on a journey before closing in a blaze of three-way guitar dueling that followed Ringo's *only* recorded drum solo. *Abbey Road* was a work to be proud of, unlike the still-uncertain *Let It Be* project.

Not long after the album's release, John offered up a song for consideration as the Beatles' next single. "Cold Turkey" pulled no punches in

detailing his kicking of a heroin addiction, but the song's directly personal account of so unsavory a topic mortified Paul, who otherwise welcomed any contribution John cared to make to the group. Miffed, Lennon issued it himself under the moniker "Plastic Ono Band," which he had used earlier for "Give Peace a Chance." For good measure, he stripped McCartney's name from the writing credit, ending a deal sustained since their teens.

Likewise, John booked a solo stadium performance in Toronto with a band featuring their Hamburg friend, Klaus Voormann, as well as Eric Clapton. John was so thrilled with their reception and the vibe that he

OPPOSITE: Undeterred by George and Ringo's unavailability, John recruited Paul into supporting the recording of his musical journal, "Ballad of John and Yoko." ABOVE: Though regarded by many as their strongest album, *Abbey Road* starkly depicted the group's fault lines: Side one featured John's preferred individual tracks, while side two's medley suite presented Paul's more ambitious leanings. Meanwhile, Ringo contributed his second composition and George rose above it all with his two finest efforts yet.

returned to London and, at the Apple office, turned in his notice, becoming the second Beatle to quit in 1969. (George had walked out during the *Let It Be* sessions, angered not at Paul but at John and his disfunctionality due to heroin use. He was talked back into the group after certain conditions were met.) Both Paul and Allen Klein registered their dismay with John's decision, with the latter insisting that no public announcement be made, lest any ongoing business negotiations go south. John agreed to the demand.

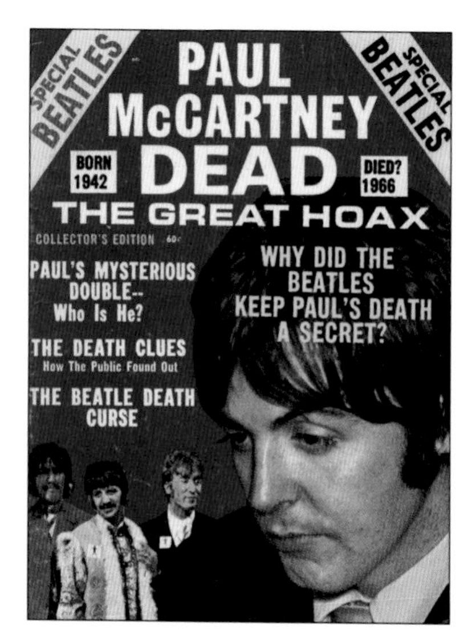

Paul took John's resignation to heart and retreated to his Scottish farm, where his uncharacteristic low profile helped fuel rumors that he had secretly died and been replaced by a lookalike (an exceptionally talented one, no doubt). The other Beatles maintained a public silence, and John—irrespective on where his position was—took the lead in producing the group's annual Christmas message to fans.

As 1970 dawned, the Beatles had a few loose ends to tidy up to prepare *Let It Be*—the album and the film—for release. On January 3, the group (minus John) gathered to record George's "I Me Mine" for the soundtrack. Not long after Paul's "Let It Be" was issued as a single, American record producer Phil Spector was called in by Klein (with John's blessing) to get an album's worth of music into releasable shape. Spector had produced John's third solo single, "Instant Karma," acquitting himself well enough to garner the invitation.

Given Spector's predilection for musical bulk—his "Wall of Sound"—it was not surprising when he applied choirs and orchestras with abandon to the Beatles' year-old, bare-bones tracks. Some songs, such as John's "Across the Universe," survived the treatment. Others, notably Paul's "The Long and Winding Road," epitomized the schmaltz that the Beatles had spent their entire career avoiding. Unsurprisingly, Paul was furious at what he saw as artistic meddling done behind his back. This was compounded when the others opposed his plan to release his own solo debut, *McCartney*, the same month that *Let It Be* was scheduled.

Ringo, the Beatle with the least animosity, was sent to Paul's house to convey the others' message. Instead of conciliation, he faced Paul's unmitigated wrath. After being asked to leave, the drummer assured John and George that perhaps it was best to let Paul have his way on this one. The two shrugged, and on April 10 promo copies of *McCartney* hit the street in the U.K., bearing a Q&A sheet. In it, Paul candidly revealed that there were no plans for him to record again with the other three. From this, the press ran with the headline "Paul Quits the Beatles." An era had ended.

"I didn't leave the Beatles—the Beatles have left the Beatles. But nobody wants to be the one to say, 'The party's over.'"

—Paul

OPPOSITE, TOP LEFT: The Beatles posed for photographers for the last time on August 22, 1969, at John's Tittenhurst Park estate. Ethan Russell shot this image, which graced 1970's *Hey Jude* compilation LP. OPPOSITE, TOP RIGHT: At the end of 1970, the Beatles gave their fans one last parting gift: *The Beatles Christmas Album,* a collection of their annual fan club holiday messages. OPPOSITE, BOTTOM: Rampant rumors that Paul had died three years earlier and been replaced swept the U.S. in the fall of 1969, giving Beatleologists the chance to comb through the group's work for "clues." LEFT: London's *Daily Mirror* notified the world to what insiders had long known: the Beatles' joyous run had come to an end.

1971–2010

INTO LEGEND

JOHN

"Yoko showed me what it was to be Elvis Beatle, and to be surrounded by sycophant slaves only interested in keeping the situation as it was—a kind of death. And that's how the Beatles ended—not because she 'split' the Beatles, but because she said to me, 'You've got no clothes on.'"

—John

Public reaction to Paul's bombshell that he was leaving the Beatles in April 1970 was one of shock and deep sadness. But the same terse statement that signaled the end of the group elicited anger from John at what he felt was Paul's betrayal. *He* had quit the Beatles first, back in September 1969, but had kept his mouth shut about it. Now, here was Paul getting all the attention—and using the publicity to sell an album, no less. John felt that Paul was thumbing his nose at him and responded in kind in the press, perpetuating the notion that the two were engaged in a blood feud.

John regarded his former group with both great fondness and deep resentment. "One has to completely humiliate oneself to be what the Beatles were," he said, but also added, "When I was a Beatle, I thought we were the best fucking group in the god-damned world." Paramount to his feelings was a sense of ownership: "I started the band. I disbanded it. It's as simple as that," he would one day claim, perhaps failing to recognize that the discussion concerned the Beatles and not the Quarry Men.

John's blind devotion to "his" group had been less of a concern after the Beatles quit touring. John was the first to make a solo record—"Give Peace a Chance"—as well as the first to perform a Beatles song publicly without the others ("Yer Blues" on the Rolling Stones' *Rock and Roll Circus* TV special in December 1968). Still, until Paul's announcement, he had kept his options open, despite telling the other Beatles that he quit just before *Abbey Road* was released. John being John meant a certain amount of shooting his mouth

John, with Yoko, leaves an immigration hearing in 1972. John's quest to stay in America despite the Nixon administration's determination to throw him out consumed his energies while impacting his art.

"Part of me suspects that I'm a loser and the other part of me thinks I'm God Almighty."

—John

ABOVE: John, seen here during the *Imagine* sessions, began his post-Beatles career working with producer Phil Spector in place of George Martin. The former speciously derided the latter as little more than an "arranger." OPPOSITE, TOP: Just months after releasing *Imagine,* John and Yoko released a holiday "evergreen," the "Happy Xmas (War Is Over)" single. OPPOSITE, BOTTOM: The public bickering between John and Paul took on a childish air when John posed with a pig, parodying Paul's *Ram* cover, and including it with the *Imagine* album. Once his ire had run its course, the image was replaced with a benign one.

off half-cocked, and the others knew him well enough not to take anything he said at face value.

The group's prolonged dissolution period exacted a deep psychological toll on all four, beginning with Paul in the wake of John's resignation, then with John following Paul's announcement. (George and Ringo's post-traumatic stress was delayed somewhat before hitting full force in the 1970s.) To cope with the breakup as well as a lifetime's worth of scarring, John spent the late spring of 1970 engaged in "primal scream" psychotherapy. As espoused by Dr. Arthur Janov, the treatment consisted of stripping away years of psychological defense mechanisms until the patient was able to revisit the original wound and express the pain with a wordless outcry: the primal scream.

Public manifestation of the experience came with John's first true solo album, released in December 1970. *John Lennon/Plastic Ono Band,* featuring Ringo on drums and Klaus Voormann on bass, was a harrowing collection of songs, each vividly personal and packing the visceral wallop of a body blow. A subtext of his own painful childhood as well as the group's breakup ran through the songs, which featured mostly one word titles such as "Isolation," "God," "Remember," and "Mother." The latter song was issued as a single with no chance of chart success, given the anguished screams that made up the coda. Still, the album was a landmark achievement.

Having gotten that out of his system, John was ready to revisit the commercial success that years of being a Beatle had acclimated him to. He reached it with *Imagine,* a set of songs anchored by the title track, which suggested to listeners the possibilities of a Utopian existence if humankind would transcend its self-imposed ideological constructs. Though some took exception to the notion of "no religion, too," while others pointed out the hypocrisy of "no possessions" coming from a couple steeped in the trappings of material wealth, there was no denying the beauty and simplicity of the tune itself. "Imagine" stands as John's signature song.

Equally noteworthy on the album was the broadside directed at his former partner. "How Do You Sleep?," a response to some subtle digs contained on Paul's prior album, was a vicious character assassination, no less so for the presence of George on the recording. Fans were stunned that a record containing such a hymn-like plea for peace could also feature such gratuitous bloodletting, but anyone surprised at such a juxtaposition coming from John Lennon simply hadn't been paying attention.

The Lennons moved to New York City not long after, and as they did, their involvement in leftist political causes increased. After issuing a gentle holiday offering, "Happy Xmas (War Is Over)" in December 1971, they

ABOVE, TOP: John followed *Imagine* with a collaboration with Yoko in June 1972, *Some Time in New York City.* This collection of topical rants damaged John's reputation just when he most needed to avoid government scrutiny. ABOVE, BOTTOM: Elephants Memory, a New York-based rock-and-boogie band, backed the Lennons on the *New York City* album as well as their August 1972 One to One charity concerts. OPPOSITE: John's recording fortunes rebounded with the issue of 1974's *Walls and Bridges,* recorded during his separation from Yoko. The album and the track "Whatever Gets You Thru the Night" reached the top of the charts.

began work on a full-length polemic, covering causes ranging from women's liberation to the troubles in Northern Ireland. The resulting *Some Time in New York City* album, packaged like a daily newspaper, probably cost John more fans than it won him with its strident tone. More importantly, it confirmed the perception felt by the Nixon administration that Lennon was a dangerous radical who needed to be deported. So began what became a three-year struggle that saw the full weight of the U.S. government coming down on the ex-Beatle.

The pressures, which included surveillance and phone taps, led Lennon to retreat from the more overt political gestures. He released a more subdued collection of tunes, *Mind Games,* in 1973. Not long after, he and Yoko separated. With personal assistant May Pang as his companion, John went west, hanging out in Los Angeles with friends such as singer Harry Nilsson, drummer Keith Moon, and a couple of former bandmates, Ringo and Paul. Things between the ex-Beatles had mellowed considerably, and there was even talk of working together again.

Though he later characterized the time apart as his "Lost Weekend," owing to some high-profile drunken escapades that included being tossed out of the Troubadour club, it was also the most prolific period of his solo career. In addition to recording an album of oldies with Phil Spector entitled *Rock 'n' Roll,* John also managed to work with several other artists, including Ringo, to whom he contributed the title cut to his *Goodnight Vienna* album. For Nilsson, he produced *Pussy Cats,* an odd blend of oldies and emotional ballads, while with Mick Jagger at the mic, he produced a track called "Too Many Cooks" that, sadly, went unreleased for decades. David Bowie sought John's support for a cover of "Across the Universe." John obliged, and in the process cowrote another song, "Fame," which became Bowie's first No. 1 single.

John likewise recorded a remake of "Lucy in the Sky with Diamonds" with Elton John, who returned the favor by dueting with him on "Whatever Gets You Thru the Night." That single became Lennon's first No. 1, which was somewhat surprising since, among the ex-Beatles, his solo career had been running the longest. It was issued on his album *Whatever Gets You Through The*

Night, John's most cohesive collection since his debut. Though the album went to No. 1, it is often overlooked today, given John's subsequent near-disownership of it after reconciling with Yoko.

John performed in public one last time on Thanksgiving evening 1974, joining Elton at Madison Square Garden before a thunderous ovation. After performing his own recent chart-topper, plus Elton's cover, he used

Fab Fact

Years after the fact, John regarded the *Two Virgins* packaging as an embarrassment that he'd rather not have in circulation. In 1974, he dispatched May Pang to the first Beatlefest convention to buy up all the loose copies she could find.

ABOVE: John's 1970s recording career came to an end with the issue of his oldies collection, *Rock 'n' Roll,* in early 1975. The project's genesis was filled with all manner of drama, from drunkenness to gunplay in the studio. OPPOSITE: John and Yoko's fifteen-month estrangement came to an end with an announcement ("The separation didn't work out") and an appearance at the Grammy Awards on March 1, 1975.

the occasion to offer up another Beatles tune, "I Saw Her Standing There." (John dedicated this Paul song to its composer.) Though he and Yoko had maintained contact during their time apart, he was not yet ready to reconcile, despite the self-generated myth that it occurred during this night.

The following month, John became the last ex-Beatle to sign the papers that officially dissolved their partnership. Present were May Pang; his son, Julian; and former Beatles roadie Mal Evans. Having cleared away all legal roadblocks, the path to working together was now unobstructed. John, in fact, made plans to join Paul in New Orleans, where Wings was preparing to record a new album. But any would-be reunion was put on hold after John unexpectedly moved back into The Dakota apartment building in New York in early 1975. The couple announced they were expecting a child not long after.

The period of Yoko's pregnancy coincided with the winding down of the court case against the Immigration and Naturalization Service. With the Nixon administration now history, Lennon's legal team was able to prove selective prosecution, and the court handed down a ruling on October 7, 1975, clearing the way to John's legal status. Two days later, on John's thirty-fifth birthday, Yoko gave birth to a boy, Sean. An elated John declared, "I feel higher than the Empire State Building."

With his recording contract now fulfilled, John decided to be the father to Sean that he hadn't been to Julian. With little fanfare, he "retired," devoting the next five years to raising his son while Yoko took care of the family's business concerns. While John would later extravagantly claim that he completely forsook music during these years, voluminous demo tapes that surfaced years later attest otherwise. No matter where the truth lay, John apparently at long last found the domestic tranquility for which he had long derided Paul McCartney.

John's unprecedented absence from the spotlight naturally provoked much speculation from the press, fans, and even his fellow ex-Beatles, with whom he maintained sporadic contact. An effort to dispel any possible ill will, lest his silence be read as indifference, came in the form of a full-page ad taken out in the New York City papers in May 1979. In a "love letter" addressed to those asking "what, when, and why," John and Yoko thanked

"When are the Beatles getting back together?"

—a fan

"When are you going back to high school?"

—John

the public for their support and love, while assuring all that "the plants are growing" and "the cats are purring." Little of substance was offered, though the note ended cryptically: "We noticed that three angels were looking over our shoulders when we wrote this!"

PAUL

"People said, 'It's a pity that such a nice thing had to come to such a sticky end.' I think that too. It is a pity. I like fairytales. I'd love it to have had the Beatles go up in a little cloud of smoke and the four of us just find ourselves in magic robes, each holding an envelope with our stuff in it."
—Paul

When John told Paul that he wanted a "divorce" from the other Beatles in September 1969, he couldn't have stunned his bandmate any more than had he actually administered a physical blow. For all their ups and downs over the previous several years, Paul was fairly certain that as long as he tolerated John's whims and decreasing interest in Beatles projects, he wouldn't place John in the position of having to choose between his band and his outside interests. That John should proactively assert his independence was a shock that bordered on trauma.

Though in retrospect it shouldn't have been all that surprising of a move, given the full array of John's non-Beatles activity, there was a certain irony in Paul's attempts to hold the Beatles together. Yes, it was he who had attempted to fill the vacuum created after Brian Epstein had died, suggesting projects, taking the lead role, and otherwise providing a task in order to engage them. And yet, Paul somehow failed to see how his own actions alienated the others from him, sowing discord.

First, there was his habit of strongly suggesting how others should play their parts on his songs. This dictating even extended to John. (In the film *Let It Be,* Paul is shown repeatedly trying to coach John on a certain guitar fill in "I've Got a Feeling," much to the latter's annoyance. Ultimately, George nailed the part.) Then there was his increasing habit of simply going off on his own to record, applying his multi-instrumental skills to the task at hand without even giving his bandmates the opportunity to contribute. For all of

The *Wings Over the World* tour (seen here at Madison Square Garden in May 1976) saw Paul and his band play before a million fans, spread over three continents. No live show by any of his fellow ex-Beatles came close to it in either numbers or sheer spectacle.

"We've all got our sides to the story; my story is that I just want us to divide it in four and go home. And then be nice to each other."

—Paul

his devotion to keeping the Beatles going, Paul displayed incredible insensitivity at times.

Still, the end of the group devastated him. He sunk into a depression, holing up at his Scottish farm, away from the others and the Apple office (where he had once maintained the most consistent presence). As rumors that he had died spread across America, he spent his days drinking or laying in bed, barely able to function. At last, Linda, his bride, had had enough of the self-pity and rallied him to get back to work, all but putting a guitar in his hands and commanding him to play.

He did indeed emerge from the darkness, and he later recounted Linda's help in song with "Maybe I'm Amazed," his first solo classic, issued on his debut, *McCartney,* in April 1970. The album had come together initially simply as a way of testing out some recording equipment he had purchased. (In fact, it contained some songs made up on the spot.) In time, he began recording the material with more care, holding secret sessions at Morgan Studios and the old Beatles stomping ground, the number two studio at EMI on Abbey Road. Indeed, most of the album had a rough hewn, a home-made quality that was the very antithesis of what was achieved on the Beatles' last studio effort. But at this juncture, Paul was not interested in repeating triumphs.

The album's reception was mixed, with many critics carping that the unfinished-sounding release was hardly worth breaking up the Beatles over. But Paul had bigger issues to worry about than pleasing rock journalists. Allen Klein, with the blessing of three ex-Beatles, had firmly established his control over Apple, something that galled Paul tremendously. It became increasingly clear that, in order to free himself from Klein's influence and regain control over his career (and finances), he would have to sue to break their legal bond. Suing Klein meant only one thing: taking Apple—and the other three—to court. After numerous attempts to talk the others into letting him go his own way went ignored, Paul had no choice.

On December 31, 1970, Paul petitioned the High Court in London to dissolve his bonds with the Beatles. He knew full well that public opinion was not on his side, as few fans could understand the legal intricacies that mandated such an act. John, George, and Ringo feigned dismay with the legal action, spinning a narrative that portrayed themselves as blindsided by Paul's suit. (Klein had quietly made the case that as a successful songwriter, artist, and producer, Paul was a company asset and should therefore not be allowed to leave.)

OPPOSITE: The bond between Paul and Linda was a strong one, as she pulled her husband out a depressive funk to launch his post-Beatles career. ABOVE: Though no one considered Linda to be a true collaborative partner for Paul in the same sense that John had been, Paul's music publisher took exception when the couple claimed an extra share of royalties for Mrs. McCartney as "cowriter."

Fab Fact

Recorded in response to Bloody Sunday—the shooting of twenty-seven civilians by British troops in Northern Ireland—"Give Ireland Back to the Irish," Wings' debut single, was banned by the BBC for its provocative political stance. Anticipating such a move, Paul recorded a lyric-less version on the flip side.

But the court saw the merit in Paul's pleading and ruled in his favor, appointing a receiver to collect the group's common kitty until all issues could be sorted out over time. The proceedings heightened the bitterness among the former bandmates, especially John, who wasted little time tearing Paul apart in the press. His landmark interview with *Rolling Stone,* later published in book form as *Lennon Remembers,* contained numerous insults directed at McCartney, among them comparing his former partner's musicality to pop crooner Engelbert Humperdinck's.

It wouldn't have suited Paul to go after John directly, though he certainly was capable. Instead, he addressed their differences in what he felt was a far more subtle manner, between the lines in the lyrics of certain songs on his sophomore release, *Ram,* issued in May 1971. One song spoke of "too many people preaching practices," while another asserted "we believe that we can't be wrong." Paul might have stopped there, but for good measure, he placed an image on the record's sleeve that depicted a pair of beetles copulating.

John rose to the occasion of the insult, responding with put-downs of Paul on the *Imagine* album, gestures that brought more shame to John than they did to his target. After a final flurry of public squabbling in the pages of *Melody Maker,* the two agreed to a truce, putting aside the venom. Besides, by that time Paul had bigger fish to fry with the start-up of his post-Beatles act. *Ram,* a tour de force, had been recorded with a pool of top-notch session musicians. But Paul still longed to maintain contact with an audience, as he had urged upon the Beatles in their waning days.

To that end, he recruited drummer Denny Seiwell, who had played on *Ram,* as well as guitarist Denny Laine, who had sung "Go Now" with the

OPPOSITE: The addition of pros Henry McCullough (*left*), Denny Seiwell (*top*), and Denny Laine (*bottom*) to Paul and Linda's nucleus ensured that Wings' development curve would be swift. LEFT: Paul was visited backstage by Ringo at the final American show of the 1976 Wings tour. ABOVE: The 1972 song "Hi Hi Hi" was banned by the BBC for encouraging drug use, an issue that—for good reason—dogged McCartney for years. A tour of Japan in 1980 was canceled when Paul was caught at the airport bringing his stash into the country, which earned him nine days in jail.

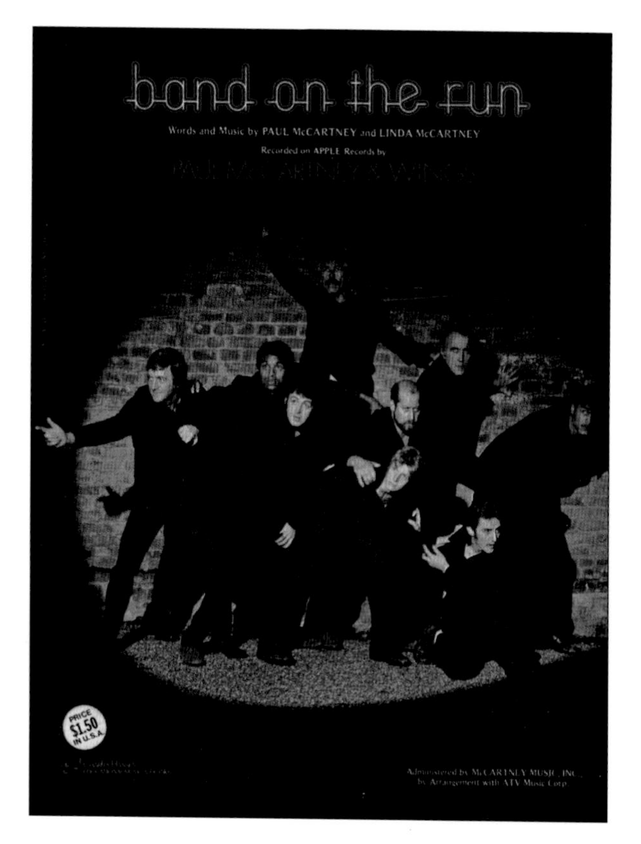

ABOVE, LEFT: *Band on the Run* was the album that fans—and critics—long hoped Paul would make. ABOVE, RIGHT: *Time* splashed Paul's image on its cover in advance of his tour, with a rendering supplied by another 1960s icon, artist Peter Max.

Moody Blues back in 1964. Along with non-musician Linda on keyboards (placed in the band at Paul's insistence), the first iteration of Wings appeared by the end of 1971. With the addition of lead guitarist Henry McCullough early in 1972, the fledgling outfit fulfilled Paul's vision of developing "organically," by way of some "hit and run" university gigs. Unannounced, the band would show up in a van and offer to play for whatever they could collect at the door. Suffice to say, students anxious to see a live Beatle turned out in force, not caring what the band sounded like.

During this time, Paul managed to get a string of singles into the charts. "Another Day," "Uncle Albert/Admiral Halsey," and "Hi Hi Hi" were hits, while songs such as "Give Ireland Back to the Irish" and "Mary Had a Little Lamb" represented his lesser efforts. By 1973, Wings had managed to find their feet and produce material worthy of their leader's talents. Hits included

"My Love," a pop standard that reached No. 1, and "Live and Let Die," a James Bond theme produced with a little help from George Martin.

Though Wings was surely but slowly finding their level, critics were less than kind to McCartney, complaining that his music lacked the artistic daring of Lennon and the gravitas of Harrison. Mostly, he was seen as an audience-pleasing middle brow: entertaining, to be sure, but one content to play to the bubblegum crowd. As for Linda, any pretense of fairness went right out the window. She was attacked mercilessly as a groupie made good, a talentless cipher whose presence alongside her immensely gifted husband was inexplicable, if not outright indefensible. But it was Paul who had demanded she be in the band, simply because she believed in him at a time when he sorely needed validation. By supporting her man, Linda subjected herself to a mountain of abuse, most of which she took in stride.

As for her bandmates, both McCullough and Seiwell took issue with a number of things, including that they were on a rather modest salary while the band scored hit records. Paul's plan to take the group to Lagos, Nigeria, to record their next album was a pipedream too many. McCullough quit, with Seiwell following days later. Undeterred, Paul simply followed through, with Wings now pared down to a threesome—the McCartneys and Laine. Paul would simply take on lead guitar and drum duties himself.

What shouldn't have worked *did*—spectacularly. Backed into a corner, the trio responded with *Band on the Run,* the album that critics long suspected but were beginning to doubt Paul had in him. Recalling *Sgt. Pepper* in some ways as an album that hung together as a start-to-finish listening experience without any explicit unifying theme, the album spawned the hits "Jet," "Helen Wheels," and the title cut, hitting No. 1 and scoring several Grammys in the process. The success put Wings on the map as rock royalty and restored Paul to his role as overachiever among the four ex-Beatles.

Part of the plan had always been to launch a global arena tour. *Band on the Run* and its follow-up, *Venus and Mars,* gave Wings the success to launch a full-scale road show. The 1975-76 Wings Over the World tour marked the high-water mark of Wingsmania, sparking the oft-told witticism that year: "Did you know that Paul McCartney was in a band before Wings?"

Fab Fact

Released at Christmastime in 1977, Wings' "Mull of Kintyre" (*pictured above*)—a campfire sing-along replete with bagpipers—became the biggest selling single in Britain with sales of more than two million, eclipsing the record set in 1963 by a song called "She Loves You."

GEORGE

"The biggest break in my career was getting in the Beatles.... The second biggest break since then is getting out of them."
—George

Within his own group, George was regarded as a junior partner. To the public he was "the quiet one," while to himself he was a "dark horse" —the "unexpectantly successful entrant." This last characterization seemed to be the most accurate in the year that the group disbanded, for with the release of his debut album, *All Things Must Pass,* George astonished the world with a collection of tunes that possessed a depth and scope that his compositions within the Beatles only hinted at. *Rolling Stone* compared the moment of this public awakening to when a famous silent screen siren made her talkie debut: "Garbo speaks" became "Harrison is free."

George had long labored in the shadow of the Lennon-McCartney songwriting team, being "allowed" to contribute his one or two tunes per album. This naturally meant, however, that as his writing proficiency developed, surplus material not afforded an outlet on a Beatles record would go unheard. Sometimes he would give away songs to friends (such as "Sour Milk Sea" to Jackie Lomax), but more often he simply stockpiled it. During the January 1969 "Get Back"/*Let It Be* project, he was bringing in finished tunes regularly. This stirred resentment from John, who often derided the compositions as he struggled with his own writer's block.

Lack of album space was one issue, but lack of respect was another. Many were the times that George's role as lead guitarist was usurped, usually by Paul but sometimes by John, an issue he accepted without complaint. At other turns, he was told what he could or could not play. "Hey Jude" was one such example, where his idea of echoing guitar lines after each sung line was summarily shot down with little finesse by Paul, who then had the lack

As George's interests in pursuing a full-time music career diminished, he increasingly devoted his energies to restoring the gardens on his sprawling Friar Park estate, a property rich in history and natural beauty.

of judgment to bring it up before the cameras in the *Let It Be* film. "I'll play what you want me to play," George responded, "or I won't play at all if you don't want me to play, you know. Whatever it is that'll please you, I'll do it."

The superior posturing from his bandmates was in contrast to the reception George received when playing with other musicians, who restored his confidence by noting his unique qualities of taste and knack for composing melodies within melodies. It is therefore of little surprise that when the end of the Beatles came, it was something close to a relief for George, who had long been made to feel straitjacketed by his limited role. Equally unsurprising is that when the time came to stretch his wings, he went big, choosing the master of the "Wall of Sound," Phil Spector, to produce his debut.

Having been through the pure pop, psychedelia, and Indian phases of his musical journey, George was embracing a simpler, almost rootsy approach by the time he began composing material for his first album. At the same time, he envisioned these basic melodies presented in Cinemascope, with platoons of musicians striving for a grandiosity that was in stark contrast to what the Beatles set out to do with the their back-to-basics approach on *Let It Be.* For George, the spiritual underpinnings to his work demanded no less. One

Fab Fact

All Things Must Pass was recorded with the help of many musicians, including several that afterward formed Derek and the Dominos with Eric Clapton. Among the then-lesser known talents heard on the record, some became famous in their own right later, including guitarist Peter Frampton, keyboardist Gary Wright, and percussionist Phil Collins.

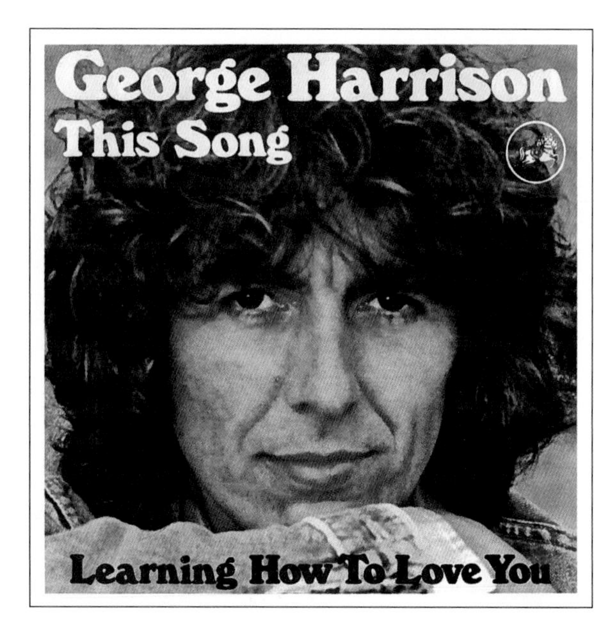

OPPOSITE, LEFT: *All Things Must Pass,* George's 1970 debut, won Grammys for Album of the Year and Record of the Year ("My Sweet Lord"). OPPOSITE, RIGHT: After the 1976 settlement of the "My Sweet Lord"/"He's So Fine" case, George turned the sour into sweet with a tongue-in-cheek send-up of the litigation, "This Song." Assuring listeners that his "expert tells me it's okay," the single became a Top Forty hit. LEFT: George's post-Beatles career included production and sideman chores for many other artists, among them Badfinger's 1971 hit, "Day After Day." He's seen here at Apple Studios, flanked by Klaus Voormann (*seated left*) and Badfinger's Pete Ham (*right*).

more ingredient became his signature sound—slide guitar—as he eschewed the usual blues licks for a voice that at times was nearly human sounding.

All Things Must Pass contained eighteen Harrisongs, spread out over two discs, with a third "bonus" disc of all-star jams thrown in. The songs ranged from the introspection of "Run of the Mill" to the thunder of "Art of Dying" to the joyous "What Is Life." But most attention surrounded a hymn inspired by the Edwin Hawkins Singers' recording of the gospel tune "Oh Happy Day," entitled "My Sweet Lord." At once catchy and uplifting, the song featured a "choir" made up of Spector and Harrison—multi-tracked many, many times—as well as a refrain that used "hallelujah" and "Hare Krishna" interchangeably. Issued as a single in late 1970, it became a massive *global* smash, easily overshadowing the work of all three of his bandmates released that year.

Unfortunately, such success stirred attention from the publishers of the Chiffons' 1963 hit "He's So Fine." Though its composer, Ronnie Mack, was long dead, its "owner" was not, and in 1971 George was sued for copyright infringement. The case became an ongoing burden, to say nothing of an embarrassment, but after it wound its way through the justice system—such as it was—in 1976 George was found liable for "subconscious plagiarism."

"I got born seemingly to become Beatle George. But it doesn't really matter who you are or what you are, because that's only a temporary sort of tag for a limited sort of period of years."

—George

"I think people who truly can live a life in music are telling the world, 'You can have my love, you can have my smiles. Forget the bad parts, you don't need them. Just take the music, the goodness, because it's the very best, and it's the part I give most willingly.'"

—George

That is, his musician's subconscious knew that the combination of chords and melody would work, even if his conscious brain did not realize where he was lifting it from. True to the workings of the secular world, the matter was settled once money had changed hands.

Still, George's lofty perch atop the rock world could barely be tainted in the wake of such success. In fact, his innate altruism was summoned in summer 1971 when his friend, sitar maestro Ravi Shankar, brought to his attention the calamity facing the people of Bangladesh in the wake of cyclones and civil war. Much the same way that Bob Geldof would stir to action years later when Ethiopians faced starvation, George was quick to respond, organizing the first large-scale relief drive by a major rock star, tapping the cachet that being a Beatle had earned him.

Though John and Paul ultimately spurned his invitation to participate, George did secure Ringo's services as well as those of Eric Clapton, Badfinger, Billy Preston, Leon Russell, and, most impressively, Bob Dylan, who had been laying low from public appearances in recent years. The event, billed as "George Harrison and Friends," raised a quarter-million dollars in a single day, as well as millions more through sales of the subsequent album and proceeds from the film. Though George later found himself liable for tax on the receipts (due to intractable government revenue offices), his pioneering

Fab Fact

George's friendship with the members of Monty Python manifested itself in many ways, most notably by his rescuing their second feature film in 1978, *Life of Brian,* by forming HandMade Films after their original financers backed out. George's reason? He simply wanted to see the movie. Eric Idle called it "the most expensive cinema ticket in history."

generosity set a high standard for the rock community's charitable endeavors.

George would crisscross America in 1974 with an undertaking dubbed the "Dark Hoarse" tour, due to the diminished condition of his vocal chords (from over-rehearsal and stress). His attempt to present a fully integrated funk/rock/world-music extravaganza proved ahead of his time, as audiences weren't particularly inclined to listen politely to Ravi Shankar's raga offerings. Still, George managed to stay true to his vision, weaving spiritual concerns and sophisticated music seamlessly in a way that made no concessions to commerciality.

The breakup of his marriage to Pattie Boyd, coupled with a slightly delayed reaction to the toll that Beatlemania had exacted upon him, led to a period of chemically enhanced lows during the mid-1970s. But George managed to bounce back, due in part to his happy courtship and subsequent marriage to Olivia Arias, an employee at the office of his record distributor at the time he set up his Dark Horse label. In 1978, Olivia gave birth to a son, Dhani, George's only child.

The family settled into a bucolic life at Friar Park, the sprawling 120-room Victorian mansion located in Henley-on-Thames. There, George indulged his love of gardening between album projects, which he created at his state-of-the-art home recording facility. Friar Park would remain his home for the rest of his earthly years.

OPPOSITE: *The Concert for Bangladesh* (1972), directed by Saul Swimmer, captured the urgency George felt to aid a nation torn by natural disaster and war. ABOVE, TOP: One unscheduled stop for 1974's *Dark Horse* tour was the White House, where George's entourage— including Billy Preston (*left*), Ravi Shankar, and George's father—took up Jack Ford's invitation to meet *his* father, the president. ABOVE, BOTTOM: Friar Park, a Victorian-era mansion, was saved from certain destruction due to years of neglect when George purchased it in 1970. The building's singular structure and grounds were showcased in his video for "Crackerbox Palace"—a song *not* about Friar Park.

RINGO

"Yes, I was in the Beatles. Yes, we made some great records together. Yes, I love those boys. But that's the end of the story."
—Ringo

The future of Ringo was considered somewhat suspect in the wake of the Beatles' dissolution. First, he was not really a songwriter. Second, he wasn't exactly thought of as a singer. As the 1970s ushered in the singer/songwriter era, this put him at a double disadvantage. Still, he had skills, he had charm, and—most importantly—he had friends, lots of them. Chief among them were George Harrison and John Lennon, both of whom were in need of a good drummer.

Resuming a familiar role with the two former bandmates was as good a way as any to ease into the post-Beatles era. But first, Ringo tackled a vanity project, virtually straight off the heels of *Abbey Road*. *Sentimental Journey* was an album of big band-era songs. Each featured a different guest arranger, running the gamut from film composer Elmer Bernstein to, closer to home, Paul McCartney. With the drummer on lead vocals, the whole thing was produced by George Martin and featured his orchestra. However, for all the evident care, the collection mystified most fans.

Undeterred, Ringo next took on country music during a brief timeout from George's *All Things Must Pass* sessions. This idiom suited him much better and, with the support of Nashville's finest musicians and songwriters, *Beaucoups of Blues* was a solid effort, offering an array of tunes that showcased Ringo very much in his comfort zone. But neither release really placed him at the center of the rock world, a place worthy of his Beatles legacy where George, at least, felt he belonged.

To that end, a more traditional single was cut. It featured Ringo in his usual role along with George, who produced, as well as Stephen Stills, Klaus

Ringo takes a breather in Paris, just after the release of the 1976 album *Ringo's Rotogravure*. At the time, there were offers topping $50 million for the Beatles to reunite, something that they all considered before ultimately rejecting.

Voormann, members of Badfinger, and others. The resulting track, "It Don't Come Easy," was credited to Ringo, though many felt that as a composition, it bore more than a little resemblance to George's work. Regarded as a gesture by George to jumpstart Ringo's career, the song fulfilled the guitarist's benevolence when it made the Top Five, establishing Ringo as another dark horse Beatles winner in the singles derby.

Another hit, "Back Off Boogaloo," followed a year later. Ringo wasn't

"Congratulations— how dare you? How about writing me a song?"

—John's celebratory telegram to Ringo after "Photograph" hit No. 1

RIGHT: The 1973 album *Ringo* achieved something that no other album by an ex-Beatle had: It spawned two chart-topping singles, "Photograph" and "You're Sixteen." OPPOSITE: After *Sentimental Journey* and *Beaucoups of Blues* made fans question whether the Beatles' former drummer could rock, he released the singles "It Don't Come Easy" and "Back Off Boogaloo," two hits that redeemed his reputation.

exactly jumping into a solo career with both feet, as he kept busy pursuing a career in film. While the Beatles were still operating, he had knocked out a couple solo film projects. But without the time commitment of his former day job, he was able to put more effort into this pursuit, first appearing in Frank Zappa's *200 Motels* followed quickly by a spaghetti western, *Blindman,* in 1972. Further, he tried his luck behind the camera by producing and directing *Born to Boogie,* a concert film/documentary on the T. Rex phenomenon that was sweeping England.

But the backbeat beckoned, and through happenstance involving Harry Nilsson, Ringo connected with producer Richard Perry, who, in his wisdom, created the setting and assembled the cast that best allowed Ringo to be Ringo. George, predictably, was on hand, cowriting a throwback-sounding ballad, "Photograph," that recalled the lush sound of Phil Spector's early productions. Less predictable was the song's traction with record buyers: It shot straight to No. 1, making the drummer the third ex-Beatle to hit the top of the charts in 1973. (John's turn would come at last a year later.)

Part of what gave the ensuing *Ringo* album such a buzz was the personnel involved: all three former bandmates (though not on the same track), plus

Fab Fact

Ringo's hit "Back Off Boogaloo" has long been rumored to be a slap at Paul for his litigation against his fellow ex-Beatles, something Ringo has long denied. Still, with such lines as "Don't pretend that you are dead" and "Everything you try to do/You know it sure sounds wasted" (a reference to Paul's marijuana habit?), the charge certainly rang true for many.

"First and foremost I am a drummer.... I didn't do it to become rich and famous. I did it because it was the love of my life."

—Ringo

Marc Bolan, the Band, and Harry Nilsson. Most of the attention directed toward the album centered on a song given to Ringo by John, the tongue-in-cheek "I'm the Greatest." Directly recalling *Sgt. Pepper,* the tune featured John on piano and harmony vocal, Billy Preston on organ, and—serendipitously—George on guitar. Though not slated to appear on the track, George happened to phone the studio while the session was going on and was urged to contribute by John, who was stuck on a segment of the arrangement.

Once George arrived, things quickly fell into place—just like the old days.

Beyond the Beatles connections, *Ringo* richly deserved its success. The smart arrangements and wise song selection—which included such self-penned tunes as the Top Ten follow-up, "Oh My My," as well as "You're Sixteen," an oldie that also went to No. 1—made the album a monster, blocked from reaching the top slot only by Elton John's *Goodbye Yellow Brick Road.* With a little help from his friends, Ringo achieved the public validation of his talents that he deserved.

With the template now set, Ringo cranked out follow-up albums that included *Goodnight Vienna* and *Ringo's Rotogravure,* though shifting musical tastes eventually brought his hot streak to an end. Also influencing his decline was the hard-partying lifestyle that he pursued with a vengeance while surrounded by fellow travelers Harry Nilsson, Keith Moon, and, for a while, John Lennon. His marriage to Maureen ended, he took up with model Nancy Andrews, and he lived like an "elegant gypsy," jet-setting between haunts in Los Angeles, Monte Carlo, London, and New York.

After performances in *That'll Be the Day* (1973), *Son of Dracula* (1974), and *Lisztomania* (1975), Ringo slowed down his cinematic efforts. He released a pair of albums that abandoned the "special guest" template, *Ringo the 4th* and *Bad Boy,* but both bombed. However, a 1978 television comedy special, titled (what else?) *Ringo,* did a good job of capturing both his acting and musical abilities. Featuring a cameo from George and the Starr himself in a dual role (playing upon Mark Twain's *The Prince and the Pauper*), the show included veteran comic actor Art Carney and an up-and-coming Carrie Fisher, fresh from *Star Wars.*

Ringo's last major film role, in a comic farce called *Caveman* (1981) opposite Dennis Quaid and Shelley Long, was memorable in one respect. On location in Mexico in 1980, Ringo met model/actress Barbara Bach on the set and was instantly smitten. A near-fatal car wreck that the two were involved in had the effect of sealing their romance, and they married in April 1981.

The drummer has credited Barbara with getting him re-engaged with music. Since the late 1980s, Ringo has regularly toured with a revolving lineup of hit-makers in Ringo's All-Starr Band.

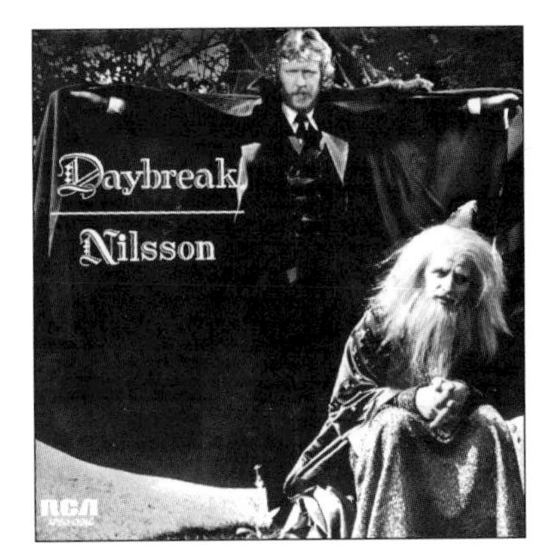

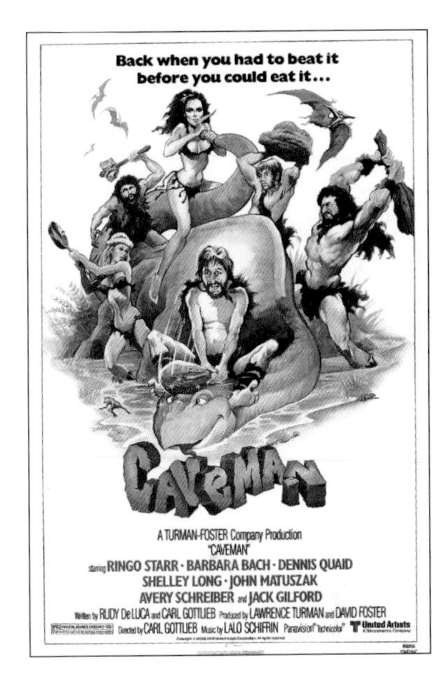

OPPOSITE: Ringo is shown in his self-titled comedy special in 1978. The show climaxed with a concert sequence, which sadly was not attempted outside the small screen. ABOVE: Ringo worked steadily in film during the 1970s. Though a couple of roles generated some acclaim, *Son of Dracula*—largely an excuse to hang out with Harry Nilsson—did not. The prehistoric farce *Caveman* consisted entirely of made-up "primitive" language.

BEATLEMANIA'S SECOND COMING

"Not the Beatles, but an incredible simulation."
—Tag line to the Broadway show Beatlemania

Though the Beatles stopped touring in 1966 and ceased operation completely in 1969, interest that went beyond mere nostalgia stayed high for the group throughout the decade after the split. While hopes that they would put aside their differences and regroup were rampant, plenty of manifestations of post-Beatlemania engaged fans throughout the 1970s, from movies and satires to plays and incredible simulations. Not bad for an act that had passed into history.

Many people too young to have experienced the group's heyday discovered the Beatles in the '70s, with many relying on their older siblings' record collections. With a void existing by the lack of any comprehensive "greatest hits," pirates and bootleggers shrewdly filled the demand. The former hawked legal recordings that had been copied or repackaged, while the latter managed to scrape together rare tracks gone unissued and live recordings, often with abysmal sound quality. In early 1973, a New Jersey firm brazenly began running ads on TV for a career-spanning "best of" called *The Beatles Alpha-Omega.*

Culled from the standard vinyl issues, the two four-record sets sold briskly until Apple execs, stirred from their slumber, slapped an injunction on them and rushed into production two "official" collections, *1962-1966* and *1967-1970*, known forever after as the "Red" and the "Blue" albums. Apple finally produced a worthy sampling of the group's best work for fans looking to freshen up their collections or (more importantly) for new fans too young to have experienced the heyday of the '60s. Later Beatles releases

Opening in London's West End in 1974, Willy Russell's *John, Paul, George, Ringo... and Bert* was a marvelous fictionalized telling of the Beatles' history, seen through the eyes of "Bert," the "fifth Beatle."

Robert Stigwood & Michael Codron presents
JOHN PAUL GEORGE
RINGO ... & BERT
by Willy Russell
DESIGN BY Anthony Sher
A Liverpool Everyman Production Directed by Alan Dosser
A MUSICAL
LYRIC THEATRE
SHAFTESBURY AVE. W.1.
TEL: 01-437 3686
SOLE LESSEES LYRIC THEATRE COMPANY LTD.

included the compilations *Rock 'N' Roll Music* and *Love Songs,* plus a live set recorded at the Hollywood Bowl.

The following year saw even greater opportunities for pushing the Beatle brand. To begin with, all four ex-Beatles either just had or were just about to score No. 1 singles—in itself making their past and present incarnations a hot property. But it was the tenth anniversary of the Beatles coming to America and appearing on *The Ed Sullivan Show* that gave the promotion a "handle." Given the reverberations of that seismic Baby Boomer event, it didn't take long for an enterprising young fan to come along and put together a formal celebration to give fans a place to commemorate what had been, for many, a life-changing experience.

"I'm all for it. I'm a Beatles fan, too!"

—John, giving his stamp of approval to Mark Lapidos for the first Beatlefest

In September 1974, Mark Lapidos organized the first Beatlefest at New York City's Commodore Hotel. The event set the pattern for all the similar gatherings that followed: flea markets containing T-shirts and all sorts of collectibles; guest speakers (usually some Beatles insider); a sound-alike band performing sets of Beatles music; and screenings of rare Beatles films. Lapidos's vision gave the fans a sense of community that has lasted to this very day.

For some, just listening to the Beatles or watching them on film wasn't enough. A pair of music entrepreneurs reasoned that an all-encompassing full immersion concert experience could take the fans to a whole new level. With platoons of well-scripted look-alikes appropriately costumed, the producers put together *Beatlemania*—a multimedia extravaganza that, for many, brought the group back to life, with music from the psychedelic era and beyond. The show hit Broadway in 1977 and ran for more than a thousand performances over the next two years. Eventually, an injunction from Apple Corps shut it down, citing appropriation of the group's likeness without permission.

The big screen was another area that seemed ripe for exploitation. An attempt to contrive a storyline by weaving together Beatles songs formed the basis of the stage musical *Sgt. Pepper's Lonely Hearts Club Band on the Road.* This bizarre fantasy, starring Peter Frampton and the Bee Gees, turned into a box office turkey in 1978. If that wasn't enough, *All This and World War II* conjoined newsreel footage of the Second World War with contemporary covers

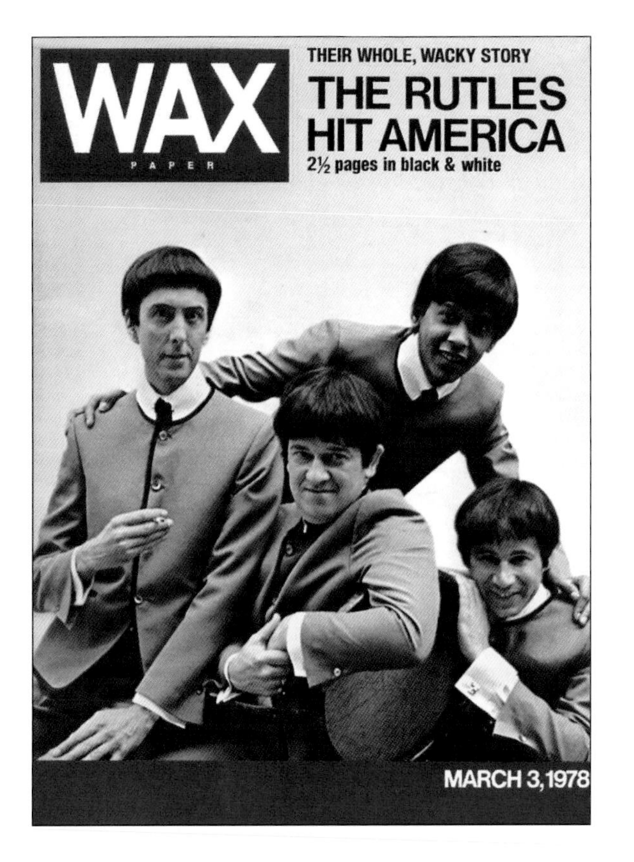

of Beatle tunes. *I Wanna Hold Your Hand,* the directorial debut of Robert Zemeckis, told the story of some young Beatles maniacs determined to witness the band's American TV debut in person.

Perhaps the most knowing account of the Beatles' history came in the form of parody, the brainstorm of Monty Python alumnus Eric Idle. *The Rutles: All You Need Is Lunch,* a critically acclaimed satire, told the story of the fictitious Rutles—a story that paralleled the Beatles' actual history, but with a satiric twist. Airing on television in 1978, the film featured dead-on musical pastiches, courtesy of former Bonzo Dog Band member Neil Innes (often called "the seventh Python"). With a cast that included many original *Saturday Night Live* cast members (as well as Mick Jagger and Paul Simon), and a cameo from George (as a reporter), the show had an air of legitimacy, as though the Beatles had sanctioned it themselves.

OPPOSITE: Now called *The Fest for Beatle Fans,* Mark and Carol Lapidos' *Beatlefest* has endured for more than thirty-five years with no signs of slowing down. ABOVE: A major outbreak of post-Beatlemania occurred in 1978, with The Rutles TV special in March followed by the less than beloved *Sgt. Pepper's Lonely Hearts Club Band* movie in July. In between lay *I Wanna Hold Your Hand,* released in April.

TWO TRAGEDIES

"John loved and prayed for the human race.
Please do the same for him."
—Yoko Ono

"George dedicated a lot of his life to obtain a good ending, and I don't
have any doubt that he was successful."
—Olivia Harrison

December 1980 saw John Lennon's Dakota apartment building abuzz with activity. After five years of commercial silence, John had decided that summer that it was time to renew his recording career, and he produced an album with Yoko that he called *Double Fantasy.* A "heart play," the record consisted of loose dialogue between man and woman, with alternating songs conveying the wide range of human emotions that accompany a romantic relationship. After the turbulence that the couple had experienced for most of their years together, ranging from the Beatles' breakup to the immigration case, the last several years had been relatively calm. They therefore believed that the time was right to share their hard-earned wisdom with the world.

With Sean now five years old, John felt ready to get back in the game. The fact that the years away had only increased his mystique meant that virtually anything he released was likely to receive a warm reception—he hoped. The LP's first single, "(Just Like) Starting Over," was a '50s-ish rocker, virtually picking up where he had left off five years before with *Rock 'n' Roll.* The reviews were generally positive, if not glowing, and the sales were quite strong. Yoko's half of the album generated some good press for its *au courant* rawness, signaling, perhaps at long last, that the public was ready to meet her halfway.

Days after John Lennon's tragic murder, a fan places flowers on a makeshift memorial just feet away from where the ex-Beatle was struck down at The Dakota.

EXTRA ● EXTRA

NEW YORK POST

METRO

JOHN LENNON SHOT DEAD

Manchester Evening News

10p TONIGHT

BEATLE GEORGE IS DEAD

KIDS IN BUS TERROR RIDE

Fab Fact

Just hours before his death, John was photographed signing the *Double Fantasy* album for the man who would end his life. In 1999, that autographed album was sold at auction for $150,000.

To that end, John spent a great deal of time after *Double Fantasy*'s release in November 1980 perfecting a Yoko composition that had been left off the album, a hypnotic dance track called "Walking on Thin Ice." It was just the thing, John believed, to launch her out of his shadow as a recording artist in her own right. On the night of December 8, the couple worked on getting the song's mix just so at the Record Plant recording studio on New York's West Side. After hours of labor, they decided to call it a night in order to see Sean before he went to sleep.

At about 10:50 P.M., their limousine arrived back at their residence. Though the sidewalk at the south entrance on 72nd Street was sometimes clotted with tourists and fans, hoping to catch a glimpse of a Beatle, at this hour it was apparently empty. Yoko exited the limo, followed by John, who carried tapes of the evening's mixes. As he made his way toward the resident's entrance a few steps behind his wife, the stillness was shattered by the exploding sound of gunshots, shattering glass, and screams. At age forty, John Lennon had been shot dead on his doorstep by a mentally unbalanced "fan" who had justified the act by asserting the ex-Beatle was a "phony"—straight out of J. D. Salinger's *Catcher in the Rye.*

Word of the killing reached most people via Howard Cosell's announcement on ABC's *Monday Night Football.* Ringo was in the Bahamas when a phone call sent the devastated drummer to New York City, where he alone out of John's former bandmates arrived in person to comfort John's widow. He was joined not long after by John's seventeen-year-old son, Julian.

Paul and George received the word separately, and each dealt with their shock and sadness by issuing statements and then going to work. Neither could face the prospect of staying still, but the enormity of the loss precluded much concentration. As for the world, literally millions faced their own grief by taking to the streets and gathering, weeping, singing, and sharing their love for a man most had never met but who had in some way touched their lives. In lieu of a funeral, Yoko requested that a vigil be held on December 14. For one last time, the world came together over John.

The 1980s were a time of heightened anxiety for the former Beatles, each of whom felt—with good reason—that they could be the next target. By

"He was a lovely guy and a very brave man and had a wonderful sense of humor. He is really just my baby brother."

—Paul, on George

the end of the decade, Paul and Ringo were ready to perform live again. Meanwhile, George was enjoying a career renaissance with the success of his *Cloud Nine* album and the spin-off super group Traveling Wilburys, which con-sisted of George, Bob Dylan, Jeff Lynne, Tom Petty, and Roy Orbison.

By the time he had lowered his profile again in 1997, the next public pronouncement from George was dire: The lifelong smoker had been diagnosed with throat cancer. Then, on December 30, 1999, a sociopath broke into the Friar Park home and stabbed George seven times before Olivia incapacitated the intruder with blows from a fireplace poker. George recovered but was on borrowed time. The cancer that he thought he had beaten spread to his lungs, and then to his brain.

Unlike John, George's slow-motion exit allowed those closest to him—which included Paul and Ringo—to say their farewells before he slipped away. The end came on November 29, 2001. At age fifty-eight, the "quiet Beatle" was gone.

OPPOSITE: After generating decades of joyous headlines, John and George's departures from the world produced these sad goodbyes. ABOVE: George and Olivia Harrison traveled the world for treatment of his cancer. Here they are in Italy in early 2001.

I'LL OFTEN STOP AND THINK ABOUT THEM

"They will always be fashionable—
the most influential pop act of all time."
—Sony Music executive Muff Winwood,
upon the 1995 release of
The Beatles Anthology

Back in the early 1990s—before George took ill—the remaining former Beatles discussed the prospect of recording some new music to accompany a lengthy documentary that would chronicle their careers. Originally titled *The Long and Winding Road,* the project's name was changed to *The Beatles Anthology,* which included a massive book that told their story in their own words. The three felt that recording anything without John wouldn't work, but in the interest of fixing a whole, they approached Yoko to see if she had any stray tapes of his that perhaps they could complete. She gave them very rough home recordings of four songs. One of them, "Free as a Bird," was unfinished but still afforded them the room to contribute.

Released in 1995 to accompany the first (of three) *Beatles Anthology* outtakes collections, the "Threetles'" take of "Free as a Bird" was a fitting tribute to both their fallen member and their own collective past. While a true reunion was never in the cards, this gift to the fans stirred deep emotions—on both ends. It was followed three months later by another track, "Real Love."

The two "new" Beatles recordings represented just some of the ways that the group's legacy has been made tangible in the decades after they disbanded. Certainly, no other rock act or cultural entity has shown the staying

When the surviving Beatles reconvened to tell their story on film and in book form, they called upon a familiar artist, Klaus Voormann, to illustrate the packaging. Klaus, with his friend Alfons Kiefer, created Beatles *Anthology* mural, a career-encompassing triptych.

THE BEATLES
The Savage Young
BEATLES
Recorded by THE BEATLES
THE BEATLES
with the beatles
BEATLES
ALL STAR SHOW
SHEA STADIUM
TUES 7:30
THE BEATLES
THE CAVERN CLUB
ETTES REMAINS
ANTHOLOGY
THE BEATLES

power or capacity for cutting across every demographic in appeal. While the four individuals started out wanting to be "bigger than Elvis," what they created was far bigger than the sum of its parts. Ensuing generations, rather than eschewing what their parents (or grandparents) loved, have instead embraced the Beatles.

As technology and the entertainment world have evolved, recent years have seen several waves of renewed popularity. One manifestation has come with the *Cirque du Soleil* show *Love*—an onstage extravaganza that blends elements of acrobatics, ballet, and Beatles music in a senses-stirring presentation by the famed French Canadian performing troupe. The idea for the Las Vegas show actually originated with George through his friendship with *Cirque* founder Guy Laliberté. Though George did not live to see it, the show's 2006 opening brought together both surviving ex-Beatles and the families of John and George for a joyous celebration, as their art was represented in yet another form. A soundtrack formed by "mash-ups"—

ABOVE: At the first anniversary of *Cirque du Soliel*'s show *Love* in June 2007, Larry King interviewed Paul and Ringo along with Yoko and Olivia. OPPOSITE: The Beatles, as seen in *Rock Band,* perform "Here Comes the Sun."

re-imaginings of their music by mixing and splicing numerous tunes together—was created for the project by George Martin and his son, Giles.

One new arena that the Beatles' reach has extended into is video gaming. Though it was a completely alien concept to Paul and Ringo, George's son, Dhani, was a game developer, and it was through his intense lobbying that *The Beatles: Rock Band* came into being. Unlike similar games, the Beatles' version necessitated the capacity for more than one singer for gamers to re-create the group's signature harmonies. As with so much else, the Beatles paved the way with this breakthrough.

"I like people having the opportunity to get to know the music from the inside out."

—Paul on *The Beatles: Rock Band*

The group's back catalog was simultaneously reexamined as well, with a team of engineers painstakingly remastering the original tapes to once again bring their music up to par with the rest of the rock world. A box set of both the stereo and mono mixes brought legions of fans around the world out in force with its release on the same day as the *Rock Band* game: 9-9-09.

Today, the Beatles remain a cultural touchstone for all ages. Their music is still in the air, and their influence on current acts is palpable. Entire families come together and celebrate the happiness their music brings at the annual Fest for Beatle Fans (as Beatlefest is now called), as musicians born long after the group ended crank out their tunes before an audience that sings the lyrics right back at them.

At fifty years, the Beatles' presence is still with us.

FIFTY FABULOUS MOMENTS

August 17, 1960: Newly named "The Beatles," the Liverpool five-some comprised of John Lennon, Paul McCartney, George Harrison, Stuart Sutcliffe, and Pete Best plays the Indra Club in Hamburg, West Germany, marking the band's first stint abroad.

October 15, 1960: The Beatles record with Ringo Starr for the first time.

November 9, 1961: Two weeks after the "My Bonnie" single is requested by Raymond Jones at the record store that Brian Epstein manages, Epstein shows up at the Cavern to see the Beatles. A month later, a management deal will be struck between the group and Brian.

June 4, 1962: The Beatles sign a recording contract with EMI's Parlophone label.

August 18, 1962: Ringo Starr officially becomes a Beatle.

October 5, 1962: "Love Me Do," the Beatles' debut single, is released on Parlophone. It will peak at No. 17 on the charts.

January 11, 1963: "Please Please Me," the group's second single, is released in Britain. It will hit No. 1 in *New Musical Express* and *Melody Maker.*

March 22, 1963: Recorded in a single day, *Please Please Me,* the Beatles' debut album, is released in Britain. It will top the charts beginning in May until displaced by *With the Beatles* in November.

April 11, 1963: "From Me to You," the group's third single, is released in Britain. It will be the first of a dozen straight chart-topping singles at home.

August 23, 1963: The Beatles release their fourth single, "She Loves You," which will become the biggest-selling single ever in the U.K.

October 13, 1963: The Beatles are watched by an estimated 15 million viewers on *Vic Parnell's Sunday Night at the London Palladium,* triggering the official outbreak of "Beatlemania."

November 22, 1963: The Beatles' second album, *With the Beatles,* is released. It eventually will displace *Please Please Me* from the top of the charts (after a run of twenty-one weeks) in the U.K.

November 29, 1963: The Beatles release their fifth single, "I Want to Hold Your Hand." It will stay at No. 1 in Britain for five straight weeks and become their best-selling single worldwide. One month later, the song will be issued by Capitol in the United States. It will hit No. 1 on February 1, where it will remain for seven weeks until displaced in March by "She Loves You."

February 9, 1964: Before 73 million viewers, the Beatles perform five songs (in two sets) on *The Ed Sullivan Show.*

March 16, 1964: The Beatles release their sixth single, "Can't Buy Me Love"/"You Can't Do That," in the United States.

April 5, 1964: *Billboard*'s Hot 100 contains *twelve* Beatle singles, including the entire Top Five: 5) "Please Please Me"; 4) "I Want to Hold Your Hand"; 3) "She Loves You"; 2) "Twist and Shout"; 1) "Can't Buy Me Love."

July 6, 1964: The Beatles' first film, *A Hard Day's Night,* premieres in Great Britain. It will open in the U.S. on August 11.

July 10, 1964: The Beatles' third album, *A Hard Day's Night,* is released in Great Britain, two weeks after appearing in a drastically different form in the United States as a soundtrack album on United Artists.

July 13, 1964: The Beatles release their seventh single, "A Hard Day's Night," in the United States.

November 23, 1964: The Beatles release their eighth single, "I Feel Fine"/ "She's a Woman," in the United States, marking the first of six straight No. 1 U.S. singles.

December 4, 1964: The Beatles' fourth album, *Beatles for Sale,* is released in Great Britain. An American counterpart, Beatles '65, will be issued on Capitol on December 15.

April 19, 1965: The Beatles release their ninth single, "Ticket to Ride"/ "Yes It Is," in the United States.

July 19, 1965: The Beatles release their tenth single, "Help!"/ "I'm Down," in the U.S.

July 29, 1965: The Beatles' second film, *Help!,* premieres in Great Britain. It will open in the U.S. on August 26.

August 6, 1965: The Beatles' fifth album, *Help!,* is released in Great Britain. The American counterpart, stripped of seven Beatles songs and filled out with incidental music, will be issued by Capitol a week later.

December 6, 1965: The Beatles release their eleventh single, "Day Tripper"/ "We Can Work It Out," in the United States, as well as their sixth album, *Rubber Soul.*

May 30, 1966: The Beatles release their twelfth single, "Paperback Writer/ "Rain," in the United States.

August 5, 1966: The Beatles release their thirteenth single, "Eleanor Rigby"/ "Yellow Submarine," in the United States, as well as their seventh album, *Revolver.*

February 13, 1967: The Beatles release their fourteenth single, "Penny Lane"/ "Strawberry Fields Forever," in the United States. It will peak at No. 2 in the U.K., thus becoming their first single to fall short of the top slot at home since "Love Me Do."

June 1, 1967: The Beatles' eighth album, *Sgt. Pepper's Lonely Hearts Club Band,* is released to worldwide acclaim.

June 25, 1967: *The Our World* satellite broadcast, depicting the Beatles recording "All You Need Is Love," is seen by more than 300 million viewers.

July 17, 1967: The Beatles release their fifteenth single, "All You Need Is Love"/"Baby You're a Rich Man," in the United States.

November 24, 1967: The Beatles release their sixteenth single, "Hello Goodbye"/ "I Am the Walrus," in the United States.

November 27, 1967: Capitol issues the LP *Magical Mystery Tour,* which includes the six songs issued in Britain as a double-EP soundtrack to their TV film as well as both sides of the year's three singles.

December 26, 1967: The Beatles' self-made television film, *Magical Mystery Tour,* is aired in Britain. Due to the nearly universal negative reaction, plans to air it in America are canceled.

March 18, 1968: The Beatles release their seventeenth single, "Lady Madonna"/ "The Inner Light," in the United States.

August 26, 1968: The Beatles release their eighteenth single, "Hey Jude"/ "Revolution," in the United States, marking—along with offerings from Mary Hopkin, Jackie Lomax, and the Black Dyke Mills Band—the debut of the Apple label. "Hey Jude" will top the charts for nine straight weeks in America.

November 13, 1968: Four months after its premiere in Britain, *Yellow Submarine*—a full-length animated feature film made up of Beatles music and likenesses—opens in America.

November 22, 1968: The Beatles release their ninth album, a self-titled two-record set called *The Beatles* (but known universally as the "White Album" due to its stark packaging).

January 13, 1969: The Beatles' tenth album, the *Yellow Submarine* soundtrack, is released in America. It contains only four previously unissued songs.

January 30, 1969: The Beatles perform a forty-five-minute lunchtime set atop their Savile Row office building, climaxing a month's worth of rehearsals and recording known as the "Get Back"/ *Let It Be* project.

May 5, 1969: The Beatles release their nineteenth single, "Get Back"/ "Don't Let Me Down," in the United States.

June 4, 1969: The Beatles release their twentieth single, "The Ballad of John and Yoko"/ "Old Brown Shoe," in the U.S.

October 1, 1969: The Beatles' eleventh—and last recorded—album, *Abbey Road,* is released in America.

October 6, 1969: The Beatles release their twenty-first single, "Something"/ "Come Together," in the United States, marking the only George composition selected as an A-side.

March 11, 1970: The Beatles release their twenty-second single, "Let It Be"/ "You Know My Name (Look Up My Number)," in the United States.

April 10, 1970: Paul tells the press that he is leaving the Beatles, signaling the group's breakup.

May 11, 1970: The final "official" U.S. Beatles single, "The Long and Winding Road"/ "For You Blue," is released.

May 13, 1970: The final Beatles motion picture, *Let It Be,* opens in New York.

May 18, 1970: The Beatles' twelfth and final album of new material, *Let It Be,* is released in America.